Balladz

Balladz

Sharon Olds

Alfred A. Knopf   New York   2022

THIS IS A BORZOI BOOK
PUBLISHED BY ALFRED A. KNOPF

www.aaknopf.com

Knopf, Borzoi Books, and the colophon are registered
trademarks of Penguin Random House LLC.

Library of Congress Cataloging-in-Publication Data
Names: Olds, Sharon, author.
Title: Balladz / Sharon Olds.
Description: First Edition. | New York : Alfred A. Knopf, 2022.
Identifiers: LCCN 2022001788 (print) | LCCN 2022001789 (ebook) |
ISBN 9780525656951 (hardcover) |
ISBN 9781524711610 (trade paperback) |
ISBN 9780525656968 (ebook)
Subjects: LCGFT: Poetry.
Classification: LCC PS3565.L34 B35 2022 (print) |
LCC PS3565.L34 (ebook) | DDC 813/.54—dc23
LC record available at https://lccn.loc.gov/2022001788
LC ebook record available at https://lccn.loc.gov/2022001789

Jacket art by Sam Messer

Manufactured in the United States of America
Published October 4, 2022
Second Printing, November 2022

for Brenda Hillman and for Robert Hass

Contents

2 Amherst Balladz

3 Balladz

4 Album from a Previous Existence

Part One

Part Two

5 Elegies

Part One

Part Two

Acknowledgments

The author wishes to thank the following publications in which a number of these poems previously appeared, sometimes in slightly different form.

"A Song Near the End of the World": *The New Yorker*
"My Head and My Mother's Breast in Quarantine Together":
    London Review of Books
"Anatomy Lesson for the Officer": *Iterant*
"Not Once": Poem-a-Day: The Poetry Foundation
"Meditation During the Sufferings and Deaths of Others":
    Prairie Schooner
"Quarantine Morning": *The Paris Review*
"339th Morning of My Easy Quarantine": *Iterant*
"X-Ray & Rats": *Prairie Schooner*
"Sprung Trap": *Iterant*
"Amherst Ballad 1": *Hunger Mountain*
"Amherst Ballad 2": *The Southern Review*
"Amherst Ballad 6": *Gulf Coast*
"Amherst Ballad 8": *The Night Heron Barks*
"Amherst Ballad 10": *Prairie Schooner*
"Best Friend Ballad": *The Threepenny Review*
"Paper Doll Ballad, for Fats": *A Gathering of the Tribes*
"Crazy Sharon Talks to the Bishop": *The American Poetry Review*
"Ballad of Once Mike Carter": *Prairie Schooner*
"Spectrum Ballad": *Hunger Mountain*
"Genesis": *Narrative*

"Bad & Crazy": *Prairie Schooner*

"Ghazal Confessional": *Gulf Coast*

"5 o'Clockface": *The Threepenny Review*

"Transformations": *The Southern Review*

"Her Brother": *The American Poetry Review*

"Wasn't Afraid Of": *Harvard Review*

"When They Say You Have Maybe Three Months Left":
    The American Poetry Review

"Heroin": *The Southern Review*

"Three Views of Him Asleep, His Final Days": *Gulf Coast*

"The Preparing": *Narrative*

"After an Epitaph on an English Headstone": *The Southern
    Review*

1
Quarantine

Quarantine Morning

Climbing the stairs, slowly, on my palms
and soles, bent far forward, I see
my shins closer than usual—
their indigo and red-violet fireworks,
their royal blue wormholes—
how much difference is there, anymore,
between me and a cadaver?
I know I won't come, after I'm dead,
though it does seem a little strange, to me,
and strange that what we learned in Seventh Grade Health
is not a structural part of each of us like heart-beat and breath,
though sometimes people die of a heart-attack in bed.
I think my mother's father did, with his mistress,
then they said to his wife he had fallen down the cellar
stairs that weren't there. I told my son that,
in his late forties, when he said I never
told him anything about my family—
and he said, What did they do then, throw him down the cellar
    stairs?
This morning, in a dream, his father came into a restaurant, I was
    waiting on the banquette
and I saw him at a distance, taller than everyone,
and with that light in the air around his face
I had seen, sometimes, when I'd arrived late to meet him.
It was not his whiteness—I had seen it around my boyfriend's face
    in high school.
With Joey I thought it was genius, inspiration almost like possession,
    and I think it was,
with my ex I thought it was goodness but I think it was sexual liking
and the illusion his tolerance for me would be lifelong.
I don't remember the last time we made love before I moved into the
    living room when I understood he was really going to leave me.
I didn't know it was the last time,

but it was like all the other times, complete, and wrenching,
though I think I said, after the series of orgasms, One more? and
   did he kiss me,
or smile, or grunt,
and I came again, although I was dead.

May 14, 2020

I lay a curse on every person of no
color who had kneeled on the throat of a person
of color. Figural or literal—
this is no
Mother May I,
I have no mother, I *am* the mother,
I am a white mother, laying
her curse. We're on the way out—if our species
lasts long enough, there will be no one of no
color. Meanwhile I curse us, for our murderous
ignorance. I have not cursed
anyone before, not my mother when she was
knapping the little knobs and tabs of my
soul off me, nor my father when he was
harming my sister. But I curse them now,
as white criminals, and I curse myself
with them. May we eat the knowledge
of suffering, may we eat the bitter
waste of the false food we have fed
others. May we eat it in pain, and in time.

My Hand

When I look at my hand, and at the back of my wrist,
gleaming with the petrolatum which I've
rubbed into its chap—mineral oil,
ceresin, lanolin, panthenol, glycerin,
bisabolol, I see the fine
wrinkles, many making diamond shapes,
some of them long cicatrice wobbles—
it looks touching to me, and lucky. And I like
the veins which bulge up from the back of my hand.
I'm a member of a couple. My partner is in
a linen shift, a pine box,
a New Hampshire earth—sacred in the Jewish
cemetery. I say to you, Carl,
my darling, it's O.K. your tissue
will melt with the dirt when spring comes,
it's O.K. you cannot change the shock-
shape of your body I love, you are innocent
of death, you are good.
We are a couple. Remember when I climbed into your narrow
hospice bed, when you could hardly move,
and as soon as I fitted myself in
along you, like the last piece of a puzzle,
we both passed out into sleep. When I drove north,
out of a city of plague, my car—
your car which you sold me for the list price—
was packed with notebooks in which our stories
are held, balanced in their slow dance
up and down and up. My epidermis
looks pretty, to me, tonight, frail
and real, like rills in sand which water
rippled. I liked to talk with you about the
golden crown the internet rabbi

said you would be wearing, after death,
at the feast. And I love, now, seeing
in the web of my glistening wrist-skin that I am
already part with thee, tender and
permanent is the night.

Quarantine

When I left the city for the house in the woods,
slowly I got to know the room where I sat
on the bed all day and looked through its arabesque foot
at the fireplace under the beveled mantel
where the oval mirror was balanced vertical,
and sometimes a brass ball cast a bent
spear of sun
onto the glass which
bounced a brilliant fish-hook onto
the ceiling. Outside the window, the worn
plastic siloes of black oil seed
dangled like the bars of a score, the songbirds in a
darting frenzy around them.
Elsewhere, people sicken and die.
Elsewhere, people starve, and thirst,
and hide by dawn, and walk by evening,
and perish, and their parents perish.
I try to hide from knowing that.
I send money, I send for a cotton
dress, for the hot weather,
for the eating and drinking and writing, describing
the luxuries of my vantage point
in plenty and safety. I do not give
enough—and my taxes are spent, by the orange
cockatoo, in the White Man House,
on bailing out bankers. O.K., spend
the rest of the day sending money
to the hungry—pay back a tithe of what
generations of my family stole.
I am of a people of thieves,
and beaters of children. I was not beaten
because of my race, but because I belonged
to my mother, and I was a girl, and a child,

and obedient—I mean sane—I never
thought of saying no to her
until I was a head taller than my mother.
And I did not deserve to be beaten, but now
I see it—I have not ever, in my life,
been beaten outside my gender, or my family, or my color.

8 Steps of 2 Steps Down

First there was a sudden rattle.
Then, loud clattering and crunching.

It seemed to be coming from below me, I went
to the top of the basement stairs and turned on the

light and turned my big feet to the
side and walked down the narrow steps

between the steep risers, and over to the tame
infernal furnace. Somewhere inside it there were

snaps and crackles and pops like the elves with
our initials on the cereal box—we born

of plenty, and ignorant of the fact.
In the morning the oil man came in his truck,

and we put on our masks and bowed to each other
in a feudal dance, and he descended. When he left,

he said a mouse had gone into the fan. Now I
know what it sounds like when someone enters the system.

After

After the quarter-ton bear walks past me,
left to right, six feet away,
I notice that now I start breathing heavily
halfway up my dozen stairs—then I
lie on the bed and pant for a while.
And the tremor is worse, so that, when I'm cooking, I am
literally throwing a few ingredients together,
salt and sugar and raw rice on the floor around my feet.
My equipment for staying alive is wearing out,
my screen when I close it leaks bone-gel on the keys,
and the skin of my forearms hangs down in watered-silk rivulets.
I think I had thought I might be spared the extreme of dying.
On one of his last nights, my darling began caroling,
mad songs, as his brain was going—wild and terrible
but funny, too, I think I thought I might
live for 100 more years to describe those solos.
And Galway—maybe I would go on and on singing him since he no
    longer could.
But when I saw, in the last portrait, Willy's eyebrow
still cocked as if hunting, attentive to something at a distance,
one canine curved, a milk-thorn in his mouth,
and the bedlinen his body was wrapped in tied at the waist in a
    powerful knot,
Willy's head emerging as a curly off-white harvest bouquet.
My mouth warbled and my eyes poured
as if from the watercolor of the blue pitcher resting on his
    winding-sheet
with the blue Thank You—Willy in his cloud
setting into the mountain.
Someday I will run out of tears—

they are honored now to be shedding for Willy and Bwindi,
and Galway and Charlie. And maybe, if I'm lucky,
Bobbie and Catherine might bundle me up for my wash-day,
wrap me in swaddling clothes and lay me
in the manger of the earth, with Carl, and Hazel.

Anatomy Lesson for the Officer

That is your head. That is your heart.
Elbow, bicep, knee, thigh.
And the valve in back of you, your behind,
I think it may be a genital part which
holds your genital part from in front.
I am not saying Go f. yourself.
You have done that. You have f'd our species.
I am saying, That is your holster, your gun,
your handcuffs. And those are his hands in your cuffs.
And that is a human throat you are kneeling
on. That is our throat, our brother's,
our son's, maybe our father's throat.
That is your mother's, your father's, your son's,
your daughter's throat. That is your daughter's throat.

My Head and My Mother's Breast in Quarantine Together

After nine months safe and well
in a room alone, I was sitting facing
the afternoon
winter sunlight,
a magnifying mirror propped
on the windowsill. Some skin over my
breastbone was swollen, I pressed down
and in, on either side of the tiny hill.
And where had I ever seen a snake
strike by flying through the air, but out of the
little half-egg mound a six-inch
viper, yellow-green, shot,
and I pushed again, and a second Worme
(medieval for a dragon) streaked.
EEUUwww, as anyone sane would say,
anyone raised by a mother who kept larvae
in jars with leaves—they named one
"Mommy's Disgusting." As a child I had seen how my
mother looked at her drunken husband,
and now I had expelled the devil, like
gangrene reptile milk from my rib-skin.
Maybe this is the pornography
the great critic sniffed out in me.
There's not much some of us can see of the world,
solo in a room, like sitting on my
mother's lap in the car, on the highway, when my
dad swerved as we passed a woman's
leg separated from her torso on the macadam
highway and my mom with angelic aplomb
turned my head into her breast.

Centipede

Woken sober supine—at the top of the wall,
along the edge of the ceiling—
the blurred, oval dark of a roof-leak
or a creature. Put on glasses, pick up
binoculars—
a jointed insect, 6 inches long,
8 inches with the fringe of its legs
oval around it,
antennae the length of its body again
at the front. If I could have spared it, if I could have
caught and released—but slept while it woke
above my open mouth? I got
the junior broom—and missed. The creature
let go,
slid down
the wall onto my bureau—it rippled,
silky and swirling, over embroider—and the
centispear of straws stabbed down,
scattering crystal and jet, and then the
acrobat swivel dancer crawled
forward away from its back two dozen
legs, and turned over slowly, in its fine
tassels. Of course I am a killer, I am
human. There had been two lives
in the apartment, now there is one. Outside
the window and down, the flame poplar
sways south and north, mourning for the earth.

Yes

Did you forget you'd killed it. Did you go back a week later
looking for it, did you pick up the coral and
turquoise necklace like the one you gave Muriel—
sea where mountain was, mountain
where sea. And the one made of the tiniest shells—
magenta, ivory, brown, from Niihau,
which Carl gave you, and the Jane Austen pendant from lucille.
Are you a ravener of your home.
When you saw the reversed teacup did you
remember the remains were under it.
Were you curious to see them. Would you look at them
with an eye eager, self-pitying, moral, aesthetic.
And how had you killed them. With a small broom used
    as a clutch of straw daggers.
And when you were in your hunting frenzy
did you feel fear, and horror, and a spear-aimer's
attention. And under the cup now do you find
a compound eye,
and labium, thread, antennae,
metathorax curved, meso
segmented, mandible palps for
biting, sucking, sipping—and some
of the hundred legs, spotted trochanter and
coxa, femur and tibia, translucent
barbed feet. Is this the one who
flowed like an oval of shadow up
the wall, a nimbus. Is it impossible
for me to be good. Is it possible for us
to try harder to kill this planet

slower. Would I kill this animal again
if it did its undulation above me
along the wall. Is this the best that I can
do this morning to work against the killing
done in my name all over the earth.

Quarantine Argiope

Some kind of egg-sac was fitted into the
angle between a 12-bevel doorframe
and the wallpaper,
by the door inside whose transom window
a herd of blue mud-dauber wasps
had commandeered a paper-wasp nest
close to the porch past which the 500-pound
bear had trudged. Today I looked closer—
something like a giant bald
bumblebee, nesting in a shell—
an inch-fat spider. With a juice glass
and a large postcard,
I trapped the glorious dancer—a female
Argiope, the one who sleeps in her
nest outdoors next to her woven

z

z

z

z

z

z

z

z's. Her dorsal pattern was like lichen,
the edges of each petal lifted—
her great omphalos back ocher,
the irregular spots cream, she drew in her
yellow legs with their bright black joints. I took her
down to the pond, laid the tumbler near a
cross-snatch loom of weeds,
and watched till she waddle-picked her way out, and
finicked up
several stems which

gave, under her massy weight.
The marks on her back were luminous:
an archer's bow pulled all the way back.
Now the first flicker of the fall
is jumping low, along the lawn,
sipping the long
worms up.
The orb spider mother is safe in the meadow.
Tomorrow her web will span a foot,
the sleep we will share rising silver in the
air around her. I could not kill her to be
sure she would not come into my room in the
middle of the night and lie down on me
to pray. I *could not* kill her now,
to prevent that.

Not Once

Not once—not when I toppled, rigid, a
5'7" pole-pine felled,
stiff as a board, a five and a half foot
plank, 16 x 32,
and not while I wallowed on the rug among
his oxygen tubes, and my cane, and his 8
wheelchair wheels, and not when I sat by his
hospice bed, chirping I'm fine!
and not the next day, when the brilliant violet
and charcoal slashed and slathered in my easy-life skin,
or days later when the purple turned yellow and the
blue green—never once when I
said No pain, Nothing broken,
did I feel lucky, did I measure the force of the
blow, the floor speeding up like a heavyweight's
smash to my cheek and eyebrow. Not until today
did I begin to feel grateful
for my good fortune—no concussion, no
fracture—as if I had expected I'd be able to be
struck by the earth, a wrecking ball,
and not feel it—
as when someone on the other side of the world,
or the city, is struck in my name, I do not feel it.

Meditation During the Sufferings
and Deaths of Others

I did not deserve to be beaten,
and I did not deserve ballet lessons—
except insofar as everyone deserves ballet lessons.
Me mum thought I was well worth beating.
She would not have thought that I deserved to starve.
I deserved the milk in her breasts—I had put it there.
When I was a baby, she withheld food to clock-train me.
She did not notice she was privileged
always to have enough food to feed her children.
And there were books in the house, I did not deserve them
except insofar as everyone deserves them.
I did not notice it was luck that I had them,
that for every book I had, someone else did not have one.
But it was not just luck that my mother beat me.
I was the second daughter of the second daughter of the second
    daughter,
the one on whom the mothers in that line
exercised their so-far sonlessness.
I did not have a second daughter,
or she was the tiny thing lost to that long-ago flu.
I did not inherit the taste for beating children
or the belief it was the only way to make them behave.
But how did I know that every soul was equal? They kept
    saying so.
And you could see it, around some people's body,
the space around it, the light in the space,
a kind of envelope, or surface tension,
as if they were whole. Those were the popular kids, the kind ones.
I did not deserve their friendship,

but sometimes I got it—because I made them laugh.

I think I was born funny—born seeing funny.

There was what they said, and what they meant, and what they did.

There was a disjunct—and it hit my funny bone,

and then like a xylophone player I hit their funny bone

and we flushed and heated and gave out the sweet percussion of our
squeaky barking.

I had the luck to earn their laughter.

But so much lies outside deserving.

I do not deserve this house.

But I do not deserve someone

breaking in and killing me.

I chose ballet lessons because I loved dancing, and the feeling, like
begging to be liked—a kind of sneaky labor.

Going to Miss Pring's garage was like walking into a church hymn and
being its turning.

What does deserve even mean? It means dessert

when you have eaten every bite on your plate.

The concept of dessert presupposes a ruler—

second daughter of a second, or not.

And when you become your own ruler?

When you rise through the dead leaves, the pieces of torn web, the
trails of slugs, when you become a guttersnipe and lift your
head and look around,

you can see the chaos,

you can choose to work toward some small justice.

I look at my life, Chaim, and I see us,

that *taste* we had for each other, and the peace

of telling each other the truth.

And we earned the peace

in the hard crib of the hospice bed, I would

climb up into it and cram myself next to you, we would murmur
    and sleep.
I like how we looked, cotyledon
fit into itself in the steel cradle like a
capsule sent out into space, to start over.

Before the Electric Traps Arrived

In the morning, there was gore on the bathroom floor,
sexagon of grout archil
red—when I looked it up I thought it was
Achilles red, like Aethelred,
as if there had been a sword fight on the tile—
gore particulate as cudbear,
the sign of a murder, there,
the trap upside down, right to left like a sturdy Hebrew letter.
So many drops of plasma the color of hematite,
the mineral form of iron oxide—
Fe_2O_3—rust,
and something between Vermilion, and Madder, and Dragon's
    Blood.
In the book, arkil red is near archaic smile,
mouse is near serpent's mound in Ohio—500 feet long—
and orkil is near Orchidopexy,
Surg., fixation of a movable testicle. I knelt to the calligraph,
I was thinking who am I less unlike, Hypatia,
executed by means of being scraped with mussel and oyster
    shells,
for being good at math,
or the *musculus*—the Muscle Mouse—
vole m., harvest m., pocket m., jumping m.
There was nothing left in the plastic jaws
but one long toenail like the bone the children held out through the
    cage-holes for the witch to finger,
and splashes of lenticular disks on the white porcelain of the toilet
    base,
each shallow saucer of dried maroon fluid like a platelet.
I kneeled in my black kimono and washed the bolt cap,
and the siphon like a snake or a kink intestine, I

bent over the liquid heavens of the underworld,
printing my knee with thistle-bait, canoe-shape, hard rodent
    turds, I
could not tell my slat from my lap, my oven from my haven,
I was a member of no congregation, I have been mass-killing the
    congregation—
no golden *déjà*, no *vu*,
no cartoon mammals named Fatso, Gusto, and Strong Mind.
Three times in my life have I felt in my heart that I had value,
three little fish, one now a 50-year-old mother,
one a man a little younger,
the third our baby who could not make it, in the dark, past the
    first three months.
When I go underground, I will hold him,
nose to tail-tip three inches, in the palm of my right hand.

Isolation Liverwurst

After a quarantine month in the woods,
no meat, no fish or eggs, just nuts,
and grains, no butter, no mayonnaise—
illness and death everywhere in the world, and me without
    mayonnaise.
Then there it was, on an online shelf, and hours
later on my back porch. And I began
to squeal, like a housewife shittin over a new
television, I danced into the kitchen
and peeled the plasticaul off, and lifted
the top slice, from its condomy ring of
casing made of the alimentary
canal of a pig,
and pressed the soft flesh up through it
and squirted a curly tail of mustard on it
and crushed the first luscious mouthful
onto my hard and soft palates with my strenuous tongue,
tasting the lips and livers and bacons
and gristles and fats, as if I was
delectating an enemy's offal,
meanwhile capering and squeaking, feeling the
salt and animal sugar and protein
blossom into my arteries,
the trimmings and crushings of Hog's Pudding.
My father's father's father was
a pig farmer, I don't know if he
prepared the ancient Roman delicacy pig vulva, I think he did
    not,
though he and his wife and his seven children were
starving, slowly, and when Childe 8,
Albert Asa, to the dark cabin came
from his mother, the newborn's father went to the
attic and ended his own life. And here I was

prancing in the quarantine to be
eating flesh of my flesh again,
devouring the plush dote-mum like a breast,
my trotters capering, my hoofs clicking on the floor.
I know about the animal packing houses
and the warming and melting of the earth, and yet I
cabrioled with meat lust like a demon
frenzying on the coffin lid of our world.
At last I am confessional,
at the time of have-not, I look at myself in this mirror.

Quarantine Fast

Today, I decided to fast, enter into a
collaboration with my fat—I will burn it,
it will give me its saved-up mayonnaise energy and white-
  frosting energy.
You know how the palms make the sign of an hourglass figure,
out for the breasts, in for the waist, out for the hips,
like a two-handed descent of a shapely body,
that's how my torso looks now, but with several curves out and in—
T, and belly, and saddlebags, and A—
a big candle left lit to sag down onto a dish,
as if I were Artemis of Ephesus,
multiple mammaries, not just in front,
but all around,
though some antiquarians say those are not tits but
bulls' testicles, or female lions' heads, what the
hell, I don't care if they are lakes of fat or
Books of Kells of fat, I say they are old girls' things, they are like
  eyes which weep milk,
and like the five huge rolls of hay—two over three—
which a truck takes by my window most days now, south to
  north.
I want to go back to being the shape of a tall chimney, with a few
  loose bricks,
some wobble on top and some wobble on the bottom,
I want to be mesomorphic like St. Augustine,
denial of chocolate, denial of the Nile wine
they drank from the paps of papyrus cups,
and St. A. would tell his stallion stories.
And later today maybe I could cook a little kale—
take a leaf from Carl's Book of Kale, his family tree of bitter and
  crisp,
and soften those green pubic kinks, and soak them in butter.

And whoever I'm sleeping with, or no one (it's no one), it is not
    useless,
and when I break my fast, it will be noticeable,
one will not have to squint to notice it.
Sometimes I sleep with a different man in my sleep every night.
Or maybe I am sleeping with God.
Or maybe I am some form of God,
sleeping each night with a different mortal man,
I who was always so faithful,
I who love faithfulness.

Narcissus Takes Another Look
at Household Tasks

In the 32nd week of solitary, safe and, well, spoiled,
I lose my verve. I'm sleeping O.K., and there are
moments of kindness in my dreams, and stretches of eros.
I'm doing sit-ups, trying to contact my core,
and tidying the dirt-floor basement—on an
unsteady wooden table, a dozen six-packs of beer
from a wedding 25 years ago.
The cardboard rips as I pick up a bottle from its recessed circle
    of dust,
thinking of the nut of my divorce mortgage—or was it the vig—
the way the attorneys—the way attorneyness
slid into the story of the house.
I tilt the green glass, and pour the slender-necked ale out into
    the sink,
it goes down inward, inward, as if against infinity.
Outside, I scrape blossoms of lichen off the inner curve of the
    granite birdbath,
and drop the latest dead mouse, maybe with milk in her breasts, I am
    so sorry, on the granite wall for a crow.
Back to the cellar for more bottles planted among the little
    vomiting batteries.
Who says the forms of art require joy?
Could not rot suffice, or anger?
The tip of my tongue with the blister on it
is a wounded feeler. From underground up,
I am like a wasted festival.
A squirrel stands up next to the wall
and puts one paw over her heart.
And me, I pledge allegiance to the sweat and salt.

Monday, November 2, 2020

The day before the next end of the world—
not the last end, not the next to last, but the one before that—
when I wake up, I lie there for an hour with my eyes closed.
It's as if, without sex, I have changed species,
but I'm not another species, I'm no species.
When I visited them, George and Mary said,
We have a view of the Golden Gate Bridge—
go in the bathroom and stand on the toilet and look out the small
    window.
8 months in isolation, I have given up on ever having a boyfriend
    again.
No touch till death—and then I won't be there for it.
All my flirtatiousness, all my seductiveness, wasted.
Yet I'm still a beggar, it's just my nature.
But I don't even beg from myself anymore.
I *just can't* have sex with myself this week, I am too bitter.
So I beg words from my friends, and drop their generous off-fall
    here.
What do I do now, that's human? I eat
(lucky), I sleep (lucky), sometimes I do something like reading—
running my eyes over language like a brush over hair.
I remember skin—another person's skin—a man's skin—
Carl's skin, above the ground,
when he breathed, his skin with its fizz of oxygen in it.
Thinking of him makes me laugh out loud with happiness!
George talked about liking plain words like *tree* and *hill*—
when we read the word, the thing appears in our mind.
The words are about themselves, and they are about their
    appearance in our minds.
This love-note keeps the time of the Monday Poets:
Joe, Matthew, Dorianne, Mike, Major.
I am the one dreaming the five—
I am in time, 5/5,

with my Muriels, my Lucilles, my Ruths, my Gwendolyns, my
    Galways.
Tomorrow the red-face devil flies over the continent, aiming his
    pitchfork.
I dare myself to have sex with myself if he loses.
I dare myself to have sex with myself if he wins.
My friends are powers, graces, truths.
And at least I am still only 77.
So many, so many, lost to us so early.
I guess we all lose everyone always, until we are ourselves lost,
but not the ones we make together.
We are a world-wide chorus in quarantine.
Much work to be done.

Quarantine Puzzle

The next morning, I woke up
with a broken thumb. Not the one
I suck, but the other one, now swollen
the color of sackbut and rust.
I went to the smalltown drugstore and said,
May I show my thumb to the doctor?
And he said, I think it is bruised,
but there could be a fair-line hachure. Later in the
day emerged some grape-color, and
gladiola mottle, on my inner
upper arm, and my left knee wasn't
working either. Meanwhile my sprained
thumb was a lurid pacifier, and the
stain on my elderly-lady crepe
bicep opulent, the surface
like spotted dick or a clayey cream
brûlée. Had I been rolled in a barrel
in the night, without a supervisor?
Had I dreamed, a day early, of the
departure of my guardian angel,
le Carré? What happened last evening? What had
been my liquid refreshment, had I
gone on a Chardonnay roundabout, had I
become a wine roustabout? Now my
thumb is fat as the earthenware teapot's
cracked spout. I have had my first blackout.

Narcissus in Quarantine

If I were an armadillo, each scale a mirror,
I could represent others instead of myself,
I could reflect multitudes.
If I were a summer horsefly,
I could soar along the wind like a green-armored dragon,
and swoop down and rescue witches from the stake,
singeing some tips of my whiskers like flexible piano-wires.
If I were a window, would I think I was the wind's eye?
If I were a very bad person,
would I think I was a good person?
If I were a roast,
would I prepare a platter in the presence of my enemies and their
    forks and knives?
If I were delicious, would I honor the horseradish?
Jesus sat in the middle of one side of the long table,
his head luminous as a light bulb with his idea of being God,
his long goddish hair tossing during the blessing.
There was rush-hour traffic of holiness around his head.
If I played God, I would play him wearing a mouse's head.
I would play him as a girl, running upstairs on all pink fours.
When I lay myself down to sleep, now,
I pray I will dream of kindness given and received,
I pray to the coils and meats of my brain
to be healed of my disbelief in my average goodness.

339th Morning of My Easy Quarantine

This morning when I woke up I had nothing,
or I felt I had nothing, but I had something—
a hangover, a lot of little somethings
like neck-ticks dispersed throughout my body,
and some gravitons too, which have risen into my flesh
and are pulling me down toward the ground—eventually into it.
I know someone important said there was not any nothing,
that a vacuum does not exist,
but when I read the arguments for and against
I could not tell which was for and which against.
There is a mush on the pond where snow and ice are
      melting,
there is no glimmer, but a gray blur,
a little yellow-blue, a little yellow-pink—like mother-of-pearl
with no glaze, no gleam, just some smudge, some scrawl,
rifts opening in the slush.
If I were closer to it, I could hear it,
murmur of departure from frozenness,
sizzle of stacks of melt.
You might have thought that I was going to yodel something
      about my interest in dulling my perceptions,
something about drying up the rich breasts of my description,
      but I am not—
though I would be talking about myself, you are used to that
      from me.
My passport has been the Chardonnay label on the bottle,
its contents have been the loop-de-loop of my fun-fair ride.
I used to think I would never throw myself away.
When I stare at the slope of snow long enough
and close my eyes, inside them I see a blazing green sphere.
When I open them again I see bright thaw-water rippling over
      the dam, I see
nothing false, nothing valueless.

X-Ray & Rats

When the X-ray of my hand came up,
sudden and skinny-boned, on the screen,
I said, through my mask, "It's—my mom's hand,"
spidery and skeletal, I saw
the mass of my big hand, around it, my
mom's little metaphysical
carpals packed in the mitt of my big-girl flesh.
I'm not going to wonder whose breast-milk
was richer—I was touched to see
the archeology of my maternal
competence. And my thumb wasn't broken, just
compromised by bruising,
inspired into crisper arthritisness, I went
out on the street as if with my hand
in my mother's. And next to the curb was a rat—
a giant, my head at the height of its thick
inflated waist. Its haunches juddered
as the hot air ran through it and kept it
rampant, fat tail along the
sidewalk, clawed feet in the street,
talons cocked, and the face fierce,
savage—no mask for a rat—front teeth
fused and turgid, canines painted on,
whiskers painted back and down
along the neck, like reins. I walked on,
and there was another, smaller, huge
rat clawing across 51st toward the
construction on the hotel where my father had
stayed once as a little executive
from the West Coast,
and then there were two more rodent effigies
menacing and shaming. I thought of my poems
about my mother—she did indeed

beat me, but had nursed me with
her full, mammal breasts, and fed me
baby food, and taken me into
gardens, and smiled when I lisped to the flowers,
and when I could stand up, I danced with them
with her blessing. I was like my mother,
and she liked that, I owe her better
than I have given her. I'm glad I don't
owe her my love, and anyway
I loved her—far more than myself.
I need to honor myself more,
so I can bless my mother.

New Year's Song

The next morning, when I remembered
that I get to keep my thumb,
they do not need to go in and break it
again, to set it,
and as for the peripheral neuropathy
in my extremities, the numbness, the tingling . . .
I very much do not want
to lose my feet—and it came to me
I love my feet.
Life is a gift, a gift given
by no one—given by nothing, as something
may be a gift of nothing, and of
the everything that nestles unknown
in nothing. For a moment the core of my life
was not desire, but the knowledge of my unearned luck.

Sprung Trap

This morning, shapely mouse turds around a forgotten
    sprung trap,
and little jet mounds of blood, and a spent match,
which turned out to be
a mouse paw and foreleg
gnawed off to free the rest of the mouse,
the tiny nails curved like multiplication in algebra.
My house has mice; the night above a summer lawn has fireflies;
    seeded rye, seeds;
I feed the mice to the crows from a piece of tinfoil on the carriage
    stone,
a series of upstate tin-footed mice,
a mouse farm. I would look for a long
time, as a child, at the picture of the hole
Stuart Little had gone into, leaving his cane outside.
In English books, boys were caned.
In my mother's house, it was a whiskered hairbrush,
its tortoise stripes beautiful as a honeybee's fur.
The first time—confirmed by independent news sources—
I was 9 months old, no brush yet, just the flat palm.
And my mother was a Stuart, she was born to it—
maenad who squeezed me out.
This morning, as a mouse farmer, I thought of Carl,
how he felt about his cows and bulls, whom he would feed, breed,
    kill, sell, castrate, and help to give birth,
sometimes his arm inside her up to his shoulder.
She to whom he was guardian.
And I thought about his father, who, as a child,
would hide in the woods with the cow, when the Gentiles came
    killing.

Spotted Aria

And then, in full, overcast, noon
light, in the old, enamel, oblong
second-floor tub, at the window—like a bathtub
high in a tree, the honey locust
just outside—I see myself,
spotted as a salamander, an
albino newt speckled with golden
oval spots (which were circles before I got
fat), and childhood freckles and specks
of cardamom, and flicks of vanilla bean and
tiny raspberry moles, and flat
scarlet petechiae. I try to
find my various markings pretty,
my stipple which would serve a sea-turtle chick
crossing a beach of chiplets of crabshell and
dark grains of trilobite cast,
and salt and pepper cranberry skin
left over from a picnic feast, and
Rhode-Island-Red down, and sunset
sand-blooming cereus.
The longer the quarantine lasts, the more I under-
stand that ancient desert one—
no wife, no husband, no lover, no child,
no friend, no equal—
who said, I am that I am. Alone,
crabby—in fact, furious—
and yet I am also the far older
god who said, I am not what I seem.
I am bathing, in clear light, this May
day, her luscious body.

When I Looked Out

my window, again, Childe
Harold of the Bright Tower—child of the
Twins—seemed to be doing a head-to-toe
shimmy. I looked in the mirror, and two
quarters of my face were missing—
from 6 to 9, and from 12 to 3,
replaced by a flag with a black-and-white
checkerboard pattern, rippling. Some of the
squares were narrowed by the faffling, some
splayed, and the whole board tilted, like slanted handwriting.
The day before, I was rubbing my half-numb
soles, and I prayed, Let me keep
my feet. On the way to the eye doctor,
there were seven lilies in the gutter. In the subway,
a woman screamed when she saw me—I *love*
your hair! Is it a wig? I'm bipolar, I'm harmless!
Me too, I said, holding my gray and
white cartoon braids out from my head.
He has birds in there! Alive! She pointed to a
towel next to a seated man,
who was petting a flicker.
From birth I was a storyteller,
and a liar, addicted to narratives.
The doctor said, That was an ophthalmic migraine,
your eyes are perfect. I kept saying, Thank you,
wanting to say, Thank you for your trouble,
I'm sorry for your loss. I hate to incon-
venience anyone—except
my mother and father, whose false good names
I have ruined. I moved to New York City
for its thousands of windows lit in the dark, the

happy families I was constellating.
But after I hauled my parents' names through
small Klieg lights like white mud—
in my 78th year, my eyes opened
a little wider to the suffering of others.

A Song Near the End of the World

for Galway Kinnell and Bobbie Bristol

Because I suddenly think of the bear—
my head jerks up—doesn't mean the bear
is near. I was here four months before I saw the bear.
Huge exhausted mammal trudged by the porch—it was the bear
Joe told me Sue had seen while she was picking berries.
Male, 500 pounds, the bear
was massive in front, and tapered toward the bare
patch on the furred almost curly truculent rear.
Such a hot midsummer, such a tired bear.
He was like a god—so much space was filled with bear.
Like a cumulonimbus come down to earth—a density of bear
with blood in him, and teeth, and a bear
liver and bear
lights. A pirate bear, a private bear, a lone bear,
it may be a father bear, it is a son bear,
a quarantine bear,
doing the essential work of his life—an endangered bear.
We did not share breath—I was behind the window, and the bear
passed on the other side of the porch rails like a bear
passing through bars of sunlight. And bears
are imprisoned now in smaller and smaller wild jails for bears.
When I stand at a bush now and pick a blackberry,
I wonder how the bear
does it, with his teeth or his bear
claws, which in my youth were bear-
mitt pastries, brown sugar embedded with poppy seeds like the
    dirt and gore in bear
hands—people were eaten by bears
every summer. My favorite part of this bear
was his velvety golden-brown bear

muzzle. Galway and I were mates, in a way—a friendship that
    could bear
strong hugs. To me, a male—bear
or human—was an unknown, like my husband, like Galway. I
    bore
many poems by Galway, and he bore
many by me. Was "The Bear"
a boy? I think so. A human being was male, then. A girl bear
might have seemed too much like a mother—what man then
    could bear
his mother. I think this song is like a mate for Galway's "Bear."
A friend at the end of the world—it is barely
known how long we can go on. A wish for the bear:
pleasure, safe cubs born
and yet to be born; ease of bear
mind; bear
heart's ease, and a dream of a bear
heaven, hills and woods of comb-born honey.

2

Amherst Balladz

Amherst Ballad 1

Let us Play - Yesterday -
I a Girl - sent East -
Pacific to Atlantic -
Chicago - Betweenst -

Change Stations there - East Side to West -
Betwixt -
Beauty Salon - Big Sister -
Must Have her Hair - Washed.

New England School - Old Mansions -
Everyone a Woman -
Some Sweet - some Noble -
Christian - Jew - Muslim -

Sally - Strome - Faiza -
And Daphne - whose note from Anon -
Waited in my Locker - Who are You?
Are you Nobody too?

One Senior had slept with her Half-Brother -
And the Girl - Dearest to me -
Had been Attempted - by her Father -
Who Was my Father -

Olive Day Bramhall - Winifred Post -
And the Seniors - Weintraub, Cynthia -
And the one I Loved the Most -
Paiewonsky, Avna.

And the Lovers - Miss Math and Miss Latin -
And Ancient - Augusta Gottfried -
Whose Approval I Craved - but she saw
Into me - beneath the impostor.

And John Stuart Mill - those Sentences
In upward Thrust each Himalay -
And the Isaac Watts Music Box -
Tart Genius - Emily.

Berries of her Quatrogon
Running down - our Chin -
Presence of - another World -
This world - within.

Cream and Honey of her Rhyme -
Tomboy Accurate
With Sling and Stone -
Palpable Hit -

God one Target - Man another -
And New England Trochee Grove -
Alive with Radical Wit - and Eros -
Salt Tongue - and Groove.

She was our Girl - our Woman -
Man enough - for me - her Will
Adamant - we held her in Earthy
Celestial Respect, where I Hold Her Still

And she moves - when Held - like an Antibody -
Holding a Virus
From the Body Politic - To Dance It
Into Bliss - of Perish.

Amherst Ballad 2

You did not Sell - the Blueing -
Nor Toil with it - Wash Day -
Yours the Cerulean
Of Sky - and Brocade -

And now the Privilege comes -
To me - to make my Way -
By Subway - Train - Bus -
Into your home - into your Room

To look under your Bed - as When -
A Child, I Woke - under Mine -
Not knowing Why - what Fear or Whim
Divine - or Profane.

There may be no Dust there -
House - become Museum -
But if there were, 'twould be the Ghosts -
Of Creatures - Parts of them -

Barbs - Feet - Legs - Knees -
Arachnid - Parcel - Be -
Like Picnic - Basket - member -
Of Cancelled - Holiday -

And now I Ride - the Rails at Ease
(Who Never Rode - for Real) -
As Pilgrim - and as Decibel -
To you, who Made - the World

Perceptible to us, and no Less
Perilous - than Temporary -
Glory of the Cannot-Be -
the "Stay!"

What Beat - or Syncopate - could tell -
My Craving for - your Tale -
If not the ravish Counterpoint -
Your Calvin - Rock - and - Roll -

Amherst Ballad 3

I Did not Shave - to Visit your Town -
Though Hirsute - was my Jaw -
But Shocked the Root of each Moustache -
And turned - its Brine - To Lye.

Thus could - approach - your Door - and Knock -
With Smooth - and Beardless - Skin -
And not - a Barb'rous - Mien - insert -
Nor Hedgehog - Porcupine.

O to have known - as Pirate Girls -
Each other's - Reckless - Truth -
Before - the Bristle - Spiked - my Chin -
And Robb'd some Virgin - Wrath.

I'd sat - with Scissors - many Years -
And Cut Out - Pretty - Things -
And Pasted them - into a Book -
And then - when age 8 - Came,

Went to the Circus - with my Class -
The Clowns stared Bold - and Clear -
Came Home and cut - each Eyelash - Off,
Tiptoe, to the Mirror -

Since any - Beauty - I could have -
Would Not be of my Visage -
But drawn or Writ on Paper -
Stricter - Hieroglyph.

I Wish - I Would - have Danced - with you -
On Wild Goose Pond - Cream of the Moon.
And now - I learn - more Truth - of you -
I Call - myself - Your Own.

Amherst Ballad 4

I Slept - in your Town - behind a Door
Which from Inside - could not be Opened -
And Dreamed - as Usual - of Death -
Desire - Ruin -

A Runaway - Truck - Hit Children -
I washed Towels - and Large - Condoms -
Which held Blood - and Shit - like my Birth Bed -
Mom a - First-time - Multipara.

And my High School - dearest friend - was in my Dream -
Virginia Borson -
Whom her BFFs called, to be cool -
Virgin Abortion.

Went - on a Bus - to Mexico -
With an Address - in her Purse -
But - on the Way - Started
To Hemorrhage.

At the End - of a Debussy Concert - I Turned
To say - Who really likes Debussy -
The Silver - Tray - of her Face - Wet
With the Hour - of Ecstasy.

Now I woke - under Eaves of Rain -
An a *pest*, an a *pest*, in Amherst -
Tro chee, I *am*, holy Scansion
Of your Beg-To-Differ.

I am going to your House - to your Room.
I am Afraid. There will be China

Painted with Blossoms - my Mother's - Delicate
Inheritance I abhor/cherish -

The Loot - of her Privilege - I want
To see as her greed's Mirror -
Not mine - as if such Beauty were not
My Truth also - my Horror -

And yet - the Painted Petals be
not Tribute - but Reminder -
of Lives of Women - Not the Poorer
The Unkinder - or Kinder -

Vetch - Nettle - on Your Street -
Wheatley - Rich - along - the Verge -
Whitman - Lolling. Mothers - and Fathers
We Thank - Howling -

Amherst Ballad 5

In one Double-Glaze Pane -
Snow-Drop Lamp -
Twice size Below -
Smaller - On Top.

Blunt and Soft of Lip -
Incandescent - Tongues -
The Angle Poised
Between Droop and Up.

Behind each, in the Window -
Each one's Nape -
Brilliant - Mortal -
Opposite.

In the Dark Morning
Not here to See
Open - Acorns -
Above the Wet Street -

Ivory-Golden
Cups pouring Out.
Gone Home -
Generous Breast.

Amherst Ballad 6

The air - was Close - the Pane - slid High -
The Sill Imbued with Dust - Gave Up
A Maple Wing - of Brussels Lace -
A Tachinid or a Horse - Fly -

A small - Half Shell - of Tree Nut Style -
Crissed with Gold - Vermicule Paths
Inside - and a Common Bottle Green Fly -
Perhaps Descended from the One who Buzzed when you Died.

My Feet will Enter - your Room - Soon -
My Body - Looming - Over Them.
I thought, at 15, that you would not like me,
Too tall too fat too dumb too ugly -

But now I have a Troupe - Motel
Wing - and Shell - Motel Flies
To whom I feel equal in the Old God's Eyes.
My Mother - Never - stayed in a Motel -

So I revel in - each Motor Hotel
As if I have a right to be Here.
Your singing called me here - it should have been
Evie, or Louise, or Bren, here -

But it is I, your humble Liege -
Hunter, Diana, Siren, Heretic -
Sister to Barbaric Yawp,
Descendant Girl - of Awkward Yawl -

Down to Earth, down to Sea.
If they couldn't Catch you
Maybe they can't
Catch me!

Amherst Ballad 7

Outside your Room - in the Wain's Coat -
Below an Outlet - in the Hall -
Rolled Pill - Armadillo
Gray - Sowbug Eden Shell.

Emerald Head Spiked with Hair
Arrows - Buzzless Fly -
Barbed Leg cocked - a Quiver
Of Harrow Bristle Thigh.

On your Desk - Oak Penshaft -
Necklaced with Pearl - Steel Nib -
Well of Crystal - Murex Ink -
Collar chased - Hachures of Sheaf.

Lines of Lumen - curve and Ascend
Your Hurricane - Lamp Throat -
Ring its Glass Mouth - and Light -
Your Counterpane Quilt.

Supine then - on Jute Matting -
I inched my Way - Under your Bed -
Sleigh of Cherry Burl. As a Child -
I would Wake - under - in in's stead.

Now Lanyard on my Wrist - from my Girl -
And Porcupine Quill and Coconut Shell
And Bead Bracelet - from Didi and Major -
And the Jane Austen Pendant - from lucille.

Rose Quartz - in Sterling - Ring -
From my Elder - Sister - Patricia -
Aquamarine - in White Gold -
From our Mother's elder Sister - Patricia.

Raiment Guard me - between Flocked
Walls near Small - White - Dress.
Chair to Match - the one I was Trussed to -
Gilt Grain - Cross-Piece of Hitchcock.

When my Mom Tied me - she fed me - by Spoon -
Alphabet Soup.
I Love being - Here alone -
For Everyone.

And Shake Sparks - of Luxury
Onto the Paper Wall - Like a Dog -
Here in your Home - Emily -
Mother of Necessity.

Amherst Ballad 8

At the center of your Room -
Like a Moth - Affixt -
Your milk–color Dress - Bodice for Head -
Wings for Skirt -

As if - you knew - we would Leave - in Space -
One of us - All in White -
To twist in the Wind - Millennia -
In a - Hothouse - Mushroom - Suit.

A Soul - can Float - a Loon - alone.
The Solar System - with its Bones
And along its Body - can Orbit -
A Fascicle - a Dropped Glove.

Thank You - for your - Company -
In Grief - in Fury - Craving - Wit -
And your Courage - Isolate
Which Honed - Desire - to Wedge.

Where Solar Wind - Begins to Stop -
You went through - Termination - Shock -
And Infundibulum - and Through
No Pasarán! -

And Solar Unconformity
Until - Permanent Momentum -
And then you Lit the White–hot Iron
Chrysanthemum.

Amherst Ballad 9

No Jack I - Nor killed a Joint -
But with Arthritic Hip and Knee
Slid - Slow - under the Bed
Of Passion's - Queen -

And saw the Underside - the Cherry
Burl, the Linen Heaven - Ceil -
The Chamber Pot - eye to eye of
Rose on Top the Covered Bowl.

And while I sat on Rushes' floor
I tried to Flee myself - arrive
At where I was - where her soul had dwelled -
Her Nest, her Hive, her Alcove,

Her work-place! Her Tools -
Geode-cluster Crystal Inkwell—
Nibs of Paper-thin Steel, pen of
Mother of Pearl.

Her Parchment Flaps - of Envelopes -
Her Table - and her Chair - Seat Silk
Horsehair - Windows Four and wide
And on a Corner—

Her Lidded Dish
For Night Water -
Her White Dress -
No Salt tear - no drop of Sweat -

i craved - with my lucille i -
To honor our sister - to Ballad
From reed Matting up toward Curves
Of her Cherry-Burl sleigh Bed.

Not alone, there - with lu -
There with C.D. and Forrest,
There with Toi, Brenda, Bob -
Every radical Troubadoure

And an Adolescent Daughter -
A Rhyming Dictionary -
With added Table of Contents
Such as "Breast Poetry" -

A cartoon face with its Tongue stuck out -
Saying *yuck!* and *blech!*
And a Footnote added, "Cat now rhymes
With Chair, I guess."

But next to "Advanced Martyrdom"
And "Offspring Are Your Toys"
Is drawn a sweet crooked smile
And happy Eyes.

So she Was in that Space - with me -
Place of Miss Dickinson's scansion
I visit in my Mind when counting out her
Dactyl, Anapest, Trochee, Iamb.

Spending weeks with Emily's Feet -
Suddenly Pictured out in the air
In the morning, fresh-woken, her naked Foot
Touching - the Floor -

Gasped and sobbed - she was a *person*!
She was a woman! Alive - inside
Herself -
Writing -

And then I did not fear her -
Her detail or Grandeur -
But began to make my Way to Her Room
To Thank her.

Amherst Ballad 10

When I came to Emily's - House - late -
I remembered the feel of my Rough - Porous -
Presence in my life - my Spirit
Accidental - Chancy-ish.

In my mother's garden - I danced with Cabbage
Roses and peonies - Hollyhock -
And Snapdragons hid Faeries -
Like the sweet -

Agony - of the Wings - between
A girl's legs. Though I did not think
Flight would be granted to me - or Eggs
Or Milk or the Knot of a Pen and Ink

Rosette one could make like a silk Coat's Frog -
Then its Panels undo -
And slip off Satin Covering -
And - Be - one's Soul.

3
Balladz

Best Friend Ballad

Sometimes I'll suddenly remember the power
of her house, and of the approach to it,
down the narrow, extreme-curve-to-the-
right street, opening onto the

somehow delicate cul-de-sac, my
best friend's
house—what?
Italianate? Ogive windows,

balconies, tile roof,
the land fallen off steep behind it to the
gradual slope to the Bay. And then
the flat stones up to her Doric

portico—between them, flowering
weeds, no ice plant, no ivy, just tiny
blossoms, then there it was, like a villa,
a little Berkeley palace, a doctor's

elegant home of safety where she was
dying, 9 years old, and I didn't
let myself realize it.
If her mother had been there, maybe I could have

asked her if I could take a nap
with my friend when she fell
asleep—but her mother
had died the day before, my job

was to not let my friend know it—

so she could die as if she had

a mother. What would I have given to
have been allowed to lie down
next to her dear skeletal body.

She still had her fine, yellow-green,
thick, sour-color hair,
as if the lead poison they'd breathed had
sharpened the chartreuse of it—

what would I have given to be
allowed to fall asleep with her
and dream, alive—what would I give
now? Nothing, I have nothing to give,

none of the luck which followed in my fortunate
life. But I pray for a sleep tonight in which,
9 and 9, we can hold each other in a
green dream.

Ballad of the Chair

When I stare at the word, and it begins to loosen
and come apart, I see it has
hair in it, and *air* in it, and
ai, and *I*. I think it was just

once, for a few hours—an after-
noon—my folks performed an arranged
marriage between their middle child
and a Hitchcock. It had no head, no arms, it had

a back and four legs, which could not walk—
like me, while I was espoused to it—
it was made of dead material which had been
living, once, still marked with the free

swim of its grain. And my relationship
with it was something new in my life,
I'd never been held down, and bound
to a thing, made equal with it. All I would have

had to do was say "I'm sorry
I poured the India ink on your bed."
We didn't have the word *no-brainer*, which has
rain in it, and *bra*, and a shriek—

aiee—but the being-tied-up was nothing
compared to the pain which she gave me with
a menstrual regularity
in that room. When my younger brother would peek in,

to see me bent to an object's angles,
the shame of it was nothing—without
physical pain, everything
was nothing. And I had not read

A Child's Book of Martyrs for nothing—
martyrs which had *art* and *tears*
in it. O.K., it warped me, it scared me, it
obsessed me—well what can you do. Some kids

have a hobby-horse, some a thing
which has been tied to them.
Maybe it's time to put my prop
to sleep, to bury it, its shape

of someone who died in a fire, and plant
a bush above it, whose rose-roots can find it as it
rots, and lets my chair leaf out
again, green bud and blossom.

Grandmother, with Parakeet

In airport waiting rooms, in Eureka,
Portland, Anchorage, Seattle, members of her
court appear to me—grim
prom attendants, old women

with mouths downturned like a rainbow, their hair
iron gray, thick, fixed in
small breaking combers, battleship
curls like works of art—I recognize

the hand of my grandmother's 1940s
Northwest hairdresser, school of arrested
surf. Out of her footbridge of a mouth
came a voice with darks and lights and liquidy

creaks, and underwater hinges, and bright brown
lollopings over creek stones
which shone. I did not know the words
whiskey voice, I knew she made jokes—

I guess they were actually sour remarks!—
in that voice. And she called me *Dearie*, it was
just what she and her covey would call
a child, but I took it as a personal endearment,

a sign of preference. My Gram was mine, she
made *crabby* and *grumpy* look good,
and she gave me a bird, like a Bible aviary,
whom I taught to say, in an amber chuckle, I love Shary.

Paper Doll Ballad, for Fats

I liked cutting out paper clothes, I
liked getting the tabs right—
girls bony as coat-hangers, the mother's
right to half-bare the child, the lower

the power half. How sorely I wanted to be
sane. What a life we are given! Sudden,
and cold, with blood on it. Ferns
and grasses, reptiles, rodents, then there we

were, with our pacifiers, in our
infant seats. What they'd had when me mum was a
dote was a laudanum-soaked rag.
But I had smuggled in my thumb,

and they did not paint it with iodine
until I was 9. And those *funny feelings*,
when I sucked it—if she hadn't, early on,
socked me for it,

I could have caressed myself off to sleep!
But at scrapbook time, biting with child
scissors along the dotted lines—
an Outfit! for skating!—I travailed without cease or

fuck to imitate the middle-class WASP, though
nothing availed to keep a best friend
alive, nothing vailed against punishment,
except, at last, to be so much taller than my

mother that if I had fought her I would have
won. So I kept cutting around
the tabs, fashioning costumes like sandwich
boards to hang onto girls. But when

the music began—all of a sudden,
8th grade, "Blueberry Hill"—
my body came alive, and moved,
and found its thrill.

Crazy Sharon Talks to the Bishop

I met the Bishop on the road
and much said he—same old porridge
I heard as a child, my little body
a "foul sty."

"Love has pitched his mansion." Maybe
Love pitched her silken tent.
Love has raised its dwelling in
the place of reproduction, which can be

fitted with a full moon device
which functions as a saving grace.
And maybe everything can be rent,
everything can be sole or whole—like an

asshole. I met a Bishop, once,
when I was a teenager mad as hell about
eternal fire and birth control.
We were sitting in my mother's living room—

for I have built my poems in
a place of fancy privilege—
I held out my fingers, and wiggled them at him,
and said, "I'm trying to make you levitate."

He was not holding his crook, or his mitered
hat, but he was wearing a shirt
of magenta Egyptian cotton, woven and
dyed only for Bishops, and I said,

thinking myself
quite the brat,
"That is the most beautiful shirt
I have ever seen, could you get me a shirt

like that?"
Not seeing the privilege
and ignorance of coming from a living room
like that.

Ballad of Once Mike Carter

I like to wear
men's shirts—
because my hands are so big—I like to roll
up the cuffs, and show a man's hands

at the end of a girl's arms. And my shoulders
so wide—in men's shirts, my shoulders look
delicate—as if a man has
taken the shirt off his back and put it

around my shoulders. Once Mike Carter,
in his letter jacket, walking between
Liz Barshay, the beauty, and me,
downhill, after a high school game,

drew us into the arms of a blossoming
fruit-tree, and kissed first her, then me,
then her, then me. She had pointed breasts
like torpedoes, two *bombes*, and Egyptian eyes, and a

red, scimitar mouth, and I had
my wit, and my little Scottish lips,
and Mike had the softest most generous mouth,
and he was our class president.

She was girl height, I was almost as tall
as Mike,
my body like a nymph's just grown up. With breaking-
open flowers around our heads,

we tasted the universe,
together,
and within that pistil thing between my
legs I broke into cherry blossom.

Cuckoo Ballad

When I was 19, I spent a night naked
in the bed of the model for the tall man in
Cuckoo's Nest—smart, fierce,
triathlete, 6'6", sweet,

protective and affectionate.
My body had been broken into, once, with my
shy consent, by his friend, the model for the
Cuckoo hero, painter from Kentucky who'd played

football for Stanford—Samurai dervish,
his pencil self-portraits were savage, he would draw
as we talked and drank coffee, he was living in his car—
it never occurred to me that he was married—

today I saw he looked not unlike
the way my beloved looked before
the cancer—so strong so solid he once
jumped into the chute beside a thousand-pound heifer

whose horn was stuck, a living shofar
he eased free and clambered back out,
the only Jewish cattle-breeder in New Hampshire.
And my red-haired blood-root deflowerer had left

the country the next day, to sit
sesshin in Japan for a year, and my darling
is going to have to enter the earth
when the cancer has eaten him to death—that once

most beautiful body. There, I'm a little
calmer. And I know what I need to do,
put on Casals unaccompanied—
and dance—unaccompanied—and groan, with him.

Joined Ballad

(on seeing a photograph in 1978 of Karol Wojtyla,
aka Pope John Paul II)

I'd been raised to believe that a man could say
if a woman could be a priest or not,
could make her own choices or not.
I had not thought
whether a pope could be cute or not.
I knew he'd been a fighter in the Polish
Resistance, and saw that he had been gorgeous,
and I'd heard he was a friend of Milosz.
Our thoughts have their own free life, I thought.
It hangs deep in his robes, a delicate
clapper at the center of a bell.
It moves when he moves, a ghostly fish in a
halo of silver seaweed, the hair
swaying in the dark and the heat, and at night,
when his eyes sleep, it stands up
in praise of God.

Snap Pants Off Like

As they step toward the court—they are 6'4",
6'6", 6'9"—
their height in relation to me is like the height
of a parent in relation to a six-year-old child, and when they

snap their warm-ups off like that,
I jump, though I was not shucked like that,
the ritual was I undressed myself
alone in her room—the bottom half.

Did I ever see anything
change as fast as their pants? Her face? I think
I never caught the moment of the change.
I have sat by a tulip, to see it turn,

on its green neck, toward the window—watched
the back of the mayfly
split as the fresh
imago humps up, spine first

and draws itself out. And the instant of sunrise—
at the center of the glow, a drop of fire casts
forth one strand
of its fur. And before first light,

in the dark, you can see—*Sie kommt!*— a tip
of the rising, waning crescent, one horn
up, and then the other. But I'd never
seen any lupine canines lower

into sight in the corners of the mouth
of my mother—
and when she died, I could not tell
just when, and it didn't matter.

Spectrum Ballad

When I looked up the spectrum, and red was the first
color, I thought of Ruth Stone's
hair, and her favorite high school sweater,
because the boys liked red sweaters—

the color which speaks of the crevices
inside the butte of the nipple,
which closes when it
stiffens—singing

its high note. And I thought of the tearful
eye of the penis, and the brilliance of the cunt's
scarlet vestibule,
and the throat, and nose, and the ear, and I thought

to think of the inside of the anus,
hold the rose window of its eros
in my mind a moment.
They said that red came first because when

white light passes through a prism
red has the longest wavelength—then orange, yellow,
green, blue, and violet the shortest.
Why didn't they put the shortest

first, or was red slowest, or oldest,
or were amber and magenta there from the start,
red among the earliest
of our ancestors, as they will outlive us
on the black earth.

Ballad of the Blossoming Branch

Maybe he had heard it before—I'm in
the habit of telling a story over
and over—and when I came to the part
at the conference, in Moscow,

when Elizabeth Hardwick was telling the story
of Robert Lowell carrying
a flowering branch of a cherry tree
from Boston across the ocean, to lay it

on Pasternak's grave, her voice tightened,
a moment, her eye and nostril gleamed,
and her hand went into her purse, under
the edge of the table, and came out again,

empty, so I put my hand in my purse,
in my lap, and touched the fold of a clean
hanky, and reached it toward her, under
the polished Russian wood,

even though I saw it was a hanky
my daughter had given me. Miss Hardwick
shook her head, as if to say—
and then my friend spoke up beside me,

a verray, parfit, gentil knyght,
and also an oak on the basepath—he said,
"To say, 'I don't want your fucking pity.'"
I got it—my stories are always about

myself. Later, I wanted to say,
But her nose was wet,
I wanted to give her what she'd sought, I did not
pity her, I revered her and wanted

to serve her, her fetch-hanky steward,
her Stuart, her Sty-warden, keeper of her
pork-kerchief unlike the one
my girl had embroidered for me in gold script "Mom's

Snot Rag." Lowell gave Pasternak
a virgin branch he cradled over
the Atlantic, I wished to give Miss Hardwick
a portion of dignity, as a beggar might

offer a favor to one who, under
the cloak of her disguise, was the queen
of heaven, who for loss of her boy
was weeping. Of course she wouldn't want

pity from me, I want to say to my
friend, or maybe from anyone, but
as for me, if you *did* pity, I'd
accept the gift, I would love your fucking pity!

Ballad of EIGHMIWAY

Then I drove by the small, local sign,
EIGHMIWAY—I used to think
it might be the name of the road-agent's daughter,
a way to spell Amy. I never drove

up it, into the woods, but after
the divorce, I would drive there with the I ♥ MICE traps,
to let the mice go, from their small
motel rooms. There was some shrieking, some horror-movie

horror as I popped a wee carrying case
and it scampered, and I would say, *Yes, my darling.*
And it came to me, with the memory
of the bucket half full of mouse pet-carriers—

I had a self, but had little sense
of self,
I was wandering through the outward appearance of a life,
displaced from my life.

He had not died, just moved ten crosstown
blocks, a half mile closer to
the first drop of the morning sun.
And did I have a moment more

of the setting moon? I kneeled at the mouth of
Eight Mile Way, and levered the miniature
garage door, and felt, as if it were
my ex's, or my own, a creature's ecstatic outburst.

Subway Ballad

Off the bus, Times Square, downpour—
heat wave—no taxi—rush hour—
suitcase—backpack—
massive briefcase—

bookbag, and the purse Billy calls
my bowling-bag carrier.
Bouncing the double-decker wheelie down
the first long flight—a young man

asked if I needed help, and easily
lifted and carried both vehicles.
Then a staircase up,
and a young man said,

"May I?" and at the top I said,
"You are my angel,"
and he looked—into my eyes
and smiled.

Another flight, another young man,
and the last stairs, a young woman.
It is what I do—be done by
by kindness.

❻ at rush hour—huge luggage
fore and aft—I apologized a lot—
we're all so sick of old white women
bragging about their helplessness.

Off at Bleecker—up elevator—
rain and urine—on its floor.
Home of privilege: faculty fortress.
At the desk, Concierge.

Up 17 floors—long view
of Lower Manhattan. My song: I want, I want
to thank you. Ask me
for anything. I hope I recognize you, fellow citizen.

Dear Stanley,

By invitation, I was underground,
talking to teachers, when our host said,
"We've brought someone here whom you want to see!"
I wildly thought at first it was you,

but it could not be, nor could it be
our student, recently leapt out of
this world, nor could it be Galway, in his too-small
hospice bed like a big cat

brought home by a child and put in a cardboard
box with a kitchen towel.
I looked over at the flight of stairs, and at the
top of it I saw the feet

the way in the hills we would see a descending
angel's feet—huge paws—
it was the bobcat mascot, like your pet from the Worcester
woods, the one from whom you learned

your loping walk. She bounced over to me, and we
hugged—her pointed-corner eyes were goldenish,
calm—the actual person's eyes
looking out through the bobcat's mouth.

I told the story of my small son
at the fair, calling out, "A Figure! A Figure!"
I did not tell of our young colleague,
the poet who, last week, took flight

from the bridge, down to the hard river,
lost to our sight, back into the woods of
the elements he had come from. Dear Stanley—dear
Figure!— I want to say, If you see him,

take Wiley
up in your arms,
and carry him, the rest of the way
over millions of years, to the undesired end of the earth.

Ballad Torn Apart

Now that I understand
that the world
as we know it
is going to end

I think of when I left my difficult lover
and went to see my friend alive
for the last time
and was driving home

and a few cars a-
head of me a
car leaped   straight up   like a cat

                                    and turned in the air
                                    and rushed past me
                                    and slammed into a solid
                                    oak behind me

                                        as if against
                                        the rush of time

                                        back to when love
                                        was being invented

                            before we spoiled the conditions for its
                            existence—land, fire, air, and water.

Geraldine Dodge Ballad

And when - on the Lists - of Festival -
Like Journey Jousts of Old -
I am not - in the First Rank -
Nor Second - but Third -

I think of all the writs I've wrote
Since Room - of Emily - was In -
And all my Privilege and Boast -
And Decades - of Entitlement -

Then count my blessings - Dodge, this year!
Which Feeds my Vanity enough -
That I am slightly less of what
I might be - such a hole - of Ass.

My Mother Margaret Annis -
Me a Whole Narcissus -
So long not grateful enough - for the Luck -
Which has preserved my Kids, my Life - good Fuck! -

Though not our Country, not our earth.
We are sore Pissed.
At the Festival - we will work -
To Resist.

Ms. Turbation

After the last orgasm, I
end up with the crown of my head in
the tricorn hat
of the floor and two walls.

Supine on the parquet I gaze
at the ceiling far away—
the angles of apartment geometry
gray and ivory.

My lower body hums, numb as if
a series of bombs has gone off,
each one having blasted a deeper
excavation than the last—stun

explosions of almost impersonal extreme
pleasure so intense the spirit heartache
of solitude seems for some time
not much to matter.

A couple of dozen corners above me—
doors, frames, ceilings, dropped
ceilings, shelves, closets,
like the reaches of an underground heaven,

and the angles are equilateral
but none looks it—
my vantage shows me isosceles,
and 45 degrees, as if,

having come apart, I see
the fractures in the crystal structure
of the hall where I hide to drive myself into this
vision inside the particle

where the pillars of matter crump and anyone's
triangular tusk ruler would shimmy
and waver in oasis shimmers
down to the horizontal. I always

thought it was love which made sex
so violent sweet,
I thought that sex hooked its wagon
to *love's* star.

Not Extinct Yet

First was the narrow harlequin fellow
at the pane. Second the glass and cardboard
to try to free it. Third was the fury
of gold legs and fan-blade wings

caught in a web, between chair rungs.
Fourth the wasp flinging itself
inches out into the air, then snapped
back by the gummed leash. Fifth

the eighth-inch, dust-colored spider darting to the
jester and back. Six the gold
stripes of the insect, six its black.
Seven the silk of enjambements cast

around it. Eight her legs walking
on it. Nine the hours of the paper-sculptor's
agony. And at the tenth hour
of my curious witness, my torment-farming—either

crush it or don't, Sharon, here at the
eleventh hour of the end of the world.

Hair Ballad

Kneeling - to the Faucet - Nape
Up - Rinsing a Foot or More
Of Hair - at the scalp, Millions -
At the tip - One Hair.

Each Eye Socket Intricate
As a Peregrine's Profile -
Unscroll the Soak Dollop Up -
And Flip - in Duplicate - one Hank

Left - a Drool Climbs the Tile -
One Right - and at a Distance, Chime
And click of Shatter. After -
Gray Bowl of Half Dome

Like a Bubble on the Floor. Touched, it's solid -
Brittle - Dust-Shod Tear -
And at a touch - Isosceles
Glass Pierce.

'Twas a Bulb - above the Sink -
Not Smithereened -
But Cut with Butcher's Grace - Crown -
For the Haggard - Checkered - Kinged -

Chased - Dressed - Check-mated - Matron
Fresh Old Maid -
Smiles into her Eyes, between
The Birth Braid - Left - and the Death Braid.

Rubber Shower Mat Ballad

When the shower mat is coming apart,
the curled flay looks like a rind
of sow, pork-belly—hundred and twenty
nipples, a pig in shit—but pigs

"are actually very clean creatures,
said the young matron," and porkers wallow
in mud for relief from biting flies.
The rubber mat, teats up,

looks like the raw, titted bacon
of a rubber industrial porcine, the rich
taps of milk remind one
of the women the dictators mutilate,

to milk a husband of information,
to husband what he knows. The Colonels—
the angels hate them. I take up the heavy
lollop, the collop of epidermis—

the fraying is on the long sides.
With kitchen shears, I cut the edges
away, making an hourglass, gray and
malleable with use, another dead goddess of the earth.

Handkerchief Ballad

I have a Vice—Accumulative—
With Cruelty connected to it.
One shape it takes—a Crewelwork Orange
Each Pore—a Stitch left Out.

Or it might make manifest a Drupe—
Cherry indigo—Cherry stone fruit—
Cherry box—Cherry limb—
Cherry alight—*cerises flambées.*

Thus my Lust—but the Labor is Manual
And Visual, the workers Children—
The cost Paid by their eyes and hands.
My mother carried several—in her Genuine

Crocodile. To me as a young
Dishevel, they were Signs of Privilege and unkept
Promises of simple Kindness.
A Stack of them—washed and folded—was

A nine-note Chord in a score—the Scene
On each the home of a Faerie—invisible
Creature—in my mother's glove-Drawer
Garden. Sewn by hungry children.

I have not bought another—but I have
Lusted After. And there was some Panky
In it—when the Pink Baseball Diamond
Arrived, the Chest-Protectors Pink,

I felt, deep inside my Abdomen—
That Girlhood Spasm, like a Faerie gulping
With emotion. It did not happen if my mother
Was anywhere around.

Not that she was a Paedophile
Though flushed exalted at Punishment time—
I think I was not her sexual but her
Corporeal Property—a Child

Worker—25¢ a week.
What my mother had with me was one thing.
What I had Apart from her was Everything
Else—the world of human Beings—

The world of the Faeries—
The world of Art and Commerce and Represen-
Tation and Friends—wise Souls like
Forrest and Karin.

Epidermis Ballad

When I'd been wearing a support sock
on my left leg—my healthy my lean
leg—and I took it off and two
ravine wrinkles had deep-incised

my ankle, the foot pinkish greenish
and cold—I rubbed the whole, lathed,
five-finial member,
and as I chafed it I saw its skin

slide like a thin covering
over the veins and muscles and fat
and the veins below, as if the skin
were a stocking, a sausage casing being

slithered over the offal—I saw that
the epithelium is the body's wet suit,
its condom, and the body the spirit's
container, its raiment. And I looked up,

and the drawer handle of the table looked like
a face, the bolts two brass eyes
and the pull a brass smile, and the back
of the frog an amber and brown pattern of

ripples like the grain of curly wood—
the way the lines of wind on water
look like growth rings on wood. And then I
got to where I was going, the sight of his

big ocher body as we paddled around
the end of the dock, washing our hair
and swimming underwater to rinse it—I would
surface dive, and see him flying

above me, buoyant and fresh, gilded
by the summer silt and pollen, not knowing that was
heaven—heaven came first, then would come
burial in the earth.

4

Album from a Previous Existence

PART ONE

If I Had Been Able

If I had been able, as an embryo,
to put my whole face into one of my
mother's pansies, I would have. As a child,
I'd squat—sitting on my heels, resting my
pointed chin on my knees, the soles of my
feet on the ground except where my arches
lifted off the dirt like the arcs of the
parhelions—and fit my small
narrow face as far as it would go
into the ardent dog satyr
visage of a *Viola kitaibeliana*,
and gaze, my short eyelashes brushing
the stamens and anthers. Although I was not
allowed to touch myself, maybe I
knew girls had a part—that part which,
even untouched, sang—descended
from a blossom. When I get my friend's note,
the bloom at the center of my body tingles
and swells, it sparkles and slightly opens.
I'm a flower as my mother was a flower, and I was made
inside her, and grew on the stem we made
together, and left through her gates which opened
below my head. I love my cunt,
and want to honor its name, the coney
in it, the rabbit in it, the cover,
the burrow, and, because it came
from inside my mother, and came through its own
mother, I want to honor my mother's
body, her lady country.

Genesis

When I was small, my mother was fun
to tell things to. She was seriously pretty,
she was anxious, and when her picture was taken
she held still
to be looked at, to be
admired, and judged. But when I was three,
and I told her, lisping, that I liked to hold
the satin binding of my blanket while I sucked
my thumb, she liked to hear that—*thucked
my thumb*—and her face softened from within.
I have her to thank that I like *telling*
things. The folder I found today
was made in 1917
of soft cardboard, lichen-embossed—
my mother was born during a world war,
like me. In the photo, she is scary pretty,
with a mouth of baby teeth, like a piglet
piranha, and her mother had spiraled the ends of her
hair into a tumble of curls,
to correct it. They corrupted my mother,
they saw her as a being more flesh
than spirit—and those eerie, sapphire
eyes—she was beautiful
like an object. I do not want to touch her,
even young as she is here,
but if I could appear to her mother right now,
then, in a guise like that of the man who
wrestled with Jacob, until the breaking
of the day—I would say to her, "Do not beat
your daughter, do not tie her up."
And I would say, to my mother's mother,

Hester, "Let me go, for the day
breaketh." And Hester would then say,
"I will not let thee go, except
thou bless me." So I blessed my mother's
mother, and my mother, and they let me go.

My Mother's Meat Grinder

Trying to believe in barometric
pressure, without recourse to mass
and gravity, I could picture it—
her bulbic tower, clamped to the breadboard which slid
out of a slot above a kitchen drawer—
her machine which ground mammalian muscle
for us to eat and prosper.
The grinder was made of stove iron, it had
a swivel top, an arm and a handle, and a
set of different sieve fronts
through which the worms of meat would ripple.
She was so tall, 5'1", and the hole in the
metal mountains from which the meat-loaf-to-
be would come was way over
my head when I'd stand in hope to be allowed
to cup my palms and receive the curly
rose-colored tresses. In summer, my mother
would send me to the school yard with a patty
of ground round, but by the time I got to the
head of the grill-line, I had eaten all
my rubies. By then I guess I knew about
animals with breasts,
who donated their lives to us, but I
don't think I remembered by then
the look of my mother's nipple when it popped
out of my brother's mouth, like a berry
with bracts, like the red jujubes of life,
the food of envy, never again
would I be allowed to nurse at God directly.

Her Portrait

The off-white curve, at the base
of each of my mother's strong stiff nails
was called a moon.
She was a terror to me.
She was what I had for softness, and she was
hard eerie. *Moon* conjures
full moon—her nail-whites not gibbous
or crescent but pointed oval, tapered at the
sides to piercey spear-blades. There was so much
sharp about my mother—the claws
of the settings holding her diamonds to her rings, her
occasional tiara, fierce Diana
double sickle, needles up,
setting into the curls her hair
was twisted to evince, bundles of apparent
romp and bounce. Permanent,
the waves were called—and in hell there was the
girl who bit her nails, who munched them like a
porcupine eating thorns.
My mom craved me to rub her back,
she felt my kindness seeking aches
in her spirit, to ease them. I loved to help her.
And now, as I limn her live portrait
with the smooth ease of a ballpoint, the ink
rolling out, the Queen of Night
glides like a gyroscope, slides along
the fine wire of her high note.
A child is a double agent—along my
spine, my mother ran up and down, as a shudder.

Bad & Crazy

At age 5, I changed schools—
Emerstink to John Manure.
The first was down the street, grim
fortress with a charcoal-colored
fire escape, the lightning zig-zag
down the side—I climbed it, one day,
in my roller skates, to hide a bully's
skate-key. The second school was up
the street and over, up and over
and up—and out of a tunnel, which ran
under it, there came a creek
downhill, between eucalyptus:
sunbeams, and water, and a sand-pebble bed
unrolling a scroll. To move from one school
to another, you had to take a test.
My mother wrote it in my Baby Book.
The test had pleased her. "Shary's evidently
unusually intelligent."
And though they did not tell me, in their minds I was no
longer insane, or stupid—
my brain, though odd, could dance like uneven
light on water, my mind was not puke
or eeuw, I had what sharp-chinned mischievous
faeries had—a little bright, little high, IQ!

When They Told Me
God Could Read My Mind,

I learned to not know
what I was thinking.
I don't know how it happened, if my mind
put its palms over its ears, so I
could not hear what was going on
in there. I summoned a blank in there.
In the same way, I called up
a ball of blaze, an oblong, hori-
zontal, flameless, heatless fire,
at the center and out almost to the edges
of my field of vision, when I was dreaming,
so I could not see what was happening.
Then I began to erase my face,
making its matter invisible,
so all someone who looked at me would
see was my spirit—no pleading eyes,
no drip WASP nose, no shut-held mouth.
I could speak unseen, as I used to intone,
in summer, from behind a pine,
"I am the pine." The men I would love
could nearly see my heart—in my eyes and in the
shock oval of my face. And what can I thank
for protecting me? It was the human
psyche in me who knew to hide me
when I needed hiding, it was my species
in me who concealed me, without asking
or telling me, it was myself
who protected me—and once I felt I could
not be seen, it could be safe to sing.

Tender Bitter

When I started having tender thoughts about
myself as a child—that long, pointed
chin, those tiny eyes—I started having
tender thoughts of my mother. She would look
up, a lot—short for an adult—
with a look of dazed longing, her fine
straight hair wrapped wet around
many small rollers, and bound back with combs
put in backward, to give her hair
some height, or with a fillet like a goddess. My hair was
loopy, soft, lollopy like
flop-eared rabbits' ears, she wrote
about it in my Baby Book, "Shar's
not conventionally beautiful—but that
naturally curly hair!" I don't think she would have
traded with me, she remembered her cold
Pilgrim mother, in my mom's sleep,
slipping the bobby-pins out of the dreaming child's
spit curls. We were big on trading—you were
supposed to want to take Jesus's place
on the cross, as he had taken yours. I *think*
my mother would have died for me—
and I think I would have died for her—
is that how the other animals do it? Who
dies for whom? My mom sometimes
liked my mind—the odd things
I said—she would write about my mind in my pink
Baby Book. She came from ignorant
educated people of self-importance
and leisure. She did not see that what I
said was funny, like joking, it was
metaphor. But it charmed her. She would not have
taken it from me, she would not have known

what to do with it, nor did she want to
mar me, as her mother had marred her. My mother . . .
loved me. If she had not beaten me,
I would have been purely enamored with her—she was so
sad, and pretty. Her eyes were a hundred
bright bright blues, like a butterfly's scales
but crystal electric, like a shattered turquoise goblet.
She did not take away my ability
to love—with her elder sister, and my elder
sister, she taught it to me. And she did not
take my mind—the one thing
of value I was born with—my mother did not
take the simile away from me.

In Praise of the Tear Glands

How do the tear glands know to make
the most tears for the strongest feelings? I was
pressing a book hard to my breastbone, and I
understood it had "broken my heart" that there
had been so little about my father I could be proud of.
Even before my sister told me
the worst thing,
there was almost nothing to be proud of.
All I could come up with was when,
next to his apartment's junior pool,
the inflated swan almost filling it,
he'd said, of his wife,
"I thought that she and I would be walking
up to the pearly gates hand in
hand together," an apology
to her for his dying first. My cheeks
were dry as I hugged the book, but as soon as I
blinked there would come
not just drops
of tears but a sheet. And when the sheet, the salt
curtain, so wet it was not very salt, it was
almost fresh, poured down—it was expressed,
the regret. I had mourned my lack of respect
even before my sister told me
the worst, but now I more fully mourned our father,
mourned his life, for a moment almost
regretted he'd been born—but if he had not,
I would not have been born, and my sister would not have been
    born.

Goodbye

When I knew he would die soon—he was still alive—
I said goodbye, for my father, to the things of this earth.
Goodbye to the goose, to its crisp skin, to its wing,
and to ham, and to brown sugar, and the glaze that
holds the light just under its surface,
gold with yellow mustard. Goodbye
to carving the ham, the way the slice
falls away in rosy suppleness,
and carving the goose, ripping off the leg,
reaching deep into the cavity to scoop out the stuffing—
goodbye to carving the bodies of the animals of this land,
to standing there, carving them sober.
And to all the turkeys you carved drunk
when I was a child, goodbye to their hacked bodies,
to all the heavy dark bottles, every
bruise on your face, every knife,
goodbye to the old life and the new life.
Goodbye to being sober, to saying
grace like a boy, bowing your head,
goodbye to your silver hair, goodbye to God,
goodbye to closing your eyes, goodbye to the
perfect, raised dome of each eyeball.
Goodbye to the pool outside that lies there in the evening
like a dish of heaven, and to the sour cigars
by the water's edge, goodbye to each crushed leaf,
each stain on your strong, dark-white teeth,
each blue curl of smoke that stands there
whole, for a moment, in the air.

What Came Next After Our Father's Death

His wife was over at the sink, there was bird-
of-paradise outside the thick
ceiling-to-floor windows, and snake plant
and elephant ear, and mother-in-law's
tongue, my father had taken a breath
and let it out, the skin of his face
glossy as a bare root, yellow-
green-white, like a bone, or an orchid
petal, he did not inhale again,
and his heart beat, and beat, without air, he was a
dead man, his heart beating,
he not breathing. Then there was a hall,
with artificial light, then
an inner room, no window, a lamp
like an oil lamp, and I was with my sister,
as if in a tomb, the windowless room
where the families sat
while the dead were dying, and then sat when the dead
had died, and my sister told me. She told me what
our father had tried to do to her once,
when he was blind drunk, maybe in a blackout,
as if he didn't know who she was,
when she was fifteen, and he had tried to go on, but she
had hid, then escaped, on the occasion of their first
and last visitation-rights
dinner, after the divorce. As she told me,
we held hands—my left her right,
her right my left, like a folk dance—
my sister, with the power to ensure
that I would not know, during his life,
the worst of our father, that I'd never know him
until he was safely dead, so that for his
whole life I had been safe from the knowledge
of him, and he had been safe from my knowledge of him.

PART TWO

Ghazal Confessional

My grandfather Cobb became fatherless
when he was one week old.

He lay in a bureau drawer. A floor
above him, in boots hole-soled,

his father's feet hung in the air
below the old hog-rope and the old

attic beam. My grandfather Cobb
was the 8th of 8 children, 8 days old,

born to a suiciding bankrupt, near where
parents, and their children, had been bought and sold.

Cobb meant testicle, and botched,
and black-backed gull.

He grew up, worked, married up,
colted, and foaled,

and he abused. And sent out his son to marry
money—hot for the folderol, cold

to the heiress.
And I was raised in that fold,

⅛ worker—pig farmer—
⅞ capitalist gold.

And for beauty and for sex and for family, I married
a descendant of the Earl of Wold.

Sharon. You thought you wanted to sing not as
one of the Cobbs, but as one of the Olds.

But out of your long life as an Olds,
you have cobbled songs, and John-Hancocked them Olds.

White Boy in Pajamas,
Big Sur Inn, Gulf War

It was startling to see him, so close to his bedtime,
a boy in pajamas with a teddy-bear print, he looked
fresh from his bath, each lop of hair
curling back, as if to caress
his Baby Shampoo head. He looked odd,
standing in the food-line with the grown-ups, and he was as
tall as a grown-up, taller than some,
though different from all of them, because of his
clean crispness, and his patterned bed-clothes—
and the shirt was not deckled all over
but only here and there, with Ursa
Minor, and with golden stars like
solar system p.j.'s, or cop
p.j.'s. Then I saw that the mammals on this
large boy's short-sleeved shirt were grizzlies—that
free-swinging hump above and behind
the lowered head—and there were only
two bears, one on each bicep,
and the star was made of real metal—
a badge—and across the fat-lump of one grizzly
was a word, all caps, like a spelling word,
s-h-e-r-i-f-f, he was an
officer in the chow line—I checked
by his hip, and there were the handcuffs, and there,
at his right hand, the worn wooden butt
of a Western handgun. Sleep, baby,
sleep. The summer woods are deep.
The boys and girls are in camo, they're away
from home, killing people, and being

killed. And yet he was a grown man,
and I remembered being his age, hitchhiking
here from privilege college,
looking for what was strange, and real,
and true as a dream, and wild as the former earth.

The Communicant

During the stretch where the train was going backward
through liquid forest, the ferns and trunks
drew back for a moment, making a glade,
and there, at its center, in a green niche,
like a saint in a glory, was a young man,
naked, his pale torso and limbs
muscled and smooth, his hair a furze around his head
which was very still, as if he were the statue of a
sacred creature, unseeing—but his hand
was moving, he seemed to be slapping his genitals
up and out, toward us, bouncing them
with deft fierceness. And he had a look of such
grievous longing, like the cry of the train,
that I did not think of the fear I'd have felt
to happen on him on my own. But he was
alone, and he seemed to have stripped himself
for a ritual, to pit himself
against the cars passing from city
to city through the dense woods, as if he
wanted to be
known to us, to be
seen, in his extreme state—
needing someone, loving and hating someone.

Bianca Helps Me Clean My Attic

When we get to the house, Bianca says,
"One can see what will trouble this sleep
of mine," and after a few hours
in the attic—grit of dust and crisp
wasps and flies and ladybugs
and ashes, she says, "Whatever sleep
it is." And when we take a break,
for coffee, she says, "Were he not gone,"
and we talk about how much we had liked
playing with our dolls. "And I think my dolls
sort of liked me," I say. "At least, I think
they didn't dislike me. What if you thought
your *dolls* disliked you, that would be mental
illness," I say. "That would be awful,"
Bianca says. "The woodchuck could say
whether it's like his long sleep,
as I describe its coming on."
We walk back up into the hot particulate
air of the past. Don't be sad,
I want to say to Bianca, you are
learning "After Apple-Picking"
with Ben, you are singing with him, the lonesome
hibernation time is gone,
the time of death in life is gone,
the air of day is yours to keep
for scores and scores of years, day
for the light, night for just some human sleep.

5 o'Clockface

When I open my eyes, there's the eastern inner
border of my home state,
the hands greenish with creamy granular
phosphorescence, and the hinge of the angle
the lake of my childhood: purple under
thunderheads; chartreuse; silver;
in sunlight the fierce turquoise of
my mother's eyes. The luminous paint has
glowed for weeks—how long since it was touched by the
light it holds. Then the furnace goes on,
like a wind in my head, an underground wind.
In my dream, my slender son was pesky—
my only dream with harshness toward him in it—
getting in my way when I wanted to work,
and I barked at him, annoyed, and lifted his
wrists over his head, the ends of his tibia and
ulna like chicken wing joints between my fingers,
and I steered him down the hall by this human boy handle
and deposited him in his room, my young
son. My first 60 years,
in my sleep I hurried not to be late
for my execution,
but since I walked away from my gorgeous
bully boyfriend, in the dark I wrangle
with people—not yet speaking truth
to power, but acting on annoyance, this time
to a tender one.
How much longer can I live without touch?
It's a sweet sentence, that at 75

"I'm between boyfriends,"
and maybe in a way I'm like a crone goddess, ish,
the Sun-Kissed Matron in gray braids,
holding my tray out to you, chest-
high, rich with night-dark California raisins.

Improv

On the morning of the drive from sea-level
to the mountain, I asked if we could stop for *melted*
cheese! at the Mexican place in Truckee.
Then I worried, does Bob think I'm a diva?
Am I always asking for things? And I thought of Toi's letter,
and I know she is the locus of a gift—
and I am too, a spiral of energy, a genie, a dust-devil,
I was born with it, a life force,
it does not belong to me, or to anyone else,
I'm the container of it, the guardian.
And I love to let it out toward people—
nectary nosegay gusts of it.
My mother would ask me to rub her back,
she said that I had Vivian Hands,
like her college best friend's—
the palms of my hands would listen for what
my mother's muscles wanted—as now,
I seem to be writing, but I'm listening for what you want,
it would be my joy to give it to you.
There is so much joy on the earth even as it is being dis-inhabited
by the other animals, and over-inhabited by us—as it is being
knocked off course and smoked and drowned.
While we have food, let us share it and eat it.
There is so much action required of us now.
And pleasure is required of us.
O my darlings, so much pleasure is required of us.

If I Were to Sing Myself,

and celebrate myself,
I would start with the fact that I wait for the pitch,
not chopping the bat, desperate, but
attending, in my Circe wheelhouse,
then circling the ash, up and back,
making the loop of a bow, which cinches
its knot when the ball is hit, and the ribbon of my
single falls between third and short.
Then I might sing my slow, portly
stroll from my towel, on the sand, toward the water,
my cellulose, my cellulite humps
and humpesses calling Matron! Matron!
(a Maiden forty pounds ago)—
flesh now rich with kisslessness,
opulent with celibacy,
bearing the actions of eating and drinking
taken against the body's craving.
And then the walking into the lake
icy with snowmelt—fully in
and under, to the pure, deaf,
wide-eyed stripes of chartreuse, navy,
and sapphire, out toward the deep center,
then the turn,
and back up the slope to the bank, the *parea*
clinging to my staggering thighs—and in rivulet snakes, down
    over the breasts,
my hair, which will dry to silver ripples.
Meanwhile, tottering on titanium femur-knobs, I'm
glistening, within and without,
then supine under the sun, so much of me, and mostly so luscious.
And when I sang my fat lament,
someone said, No, not fat—

zaftig! Rubenesque! and I thought,
Ithyphalliques et pioupiesques! And I
strode to the fire and the wine, my feet
touching, in their worn sandals,
the pink snow-tips of the sugar-packed peaks.

Into Tahoe

Then I couldn't remember what water is made of.
Maybe mineral, worked
and softened, over time. The agate of it,
closely rippled, golden, parts without
difficulty, to permit my foot
down and in, and now the whole
semi-solid of the lake is misshapen,
cut into by this human appendage.
Where has the water gone which my thick
twig has displaced? Then the other foot, then the
wading, into the stone cold.
Knees, thighs, life-shock of the sex—
slowly, from the soles up, the bottom
half of a creature is appearing in the water as if
lowered down, out of the sky.
Moment of the waist!—surface of Tahoe
ringing it, the lower torso and
legs enclosed in the ice-water skirt.
And now the danger approaches the ribs,
from the half-loops up, and now alpine frigor has the
lungs and heart in clean attack,
the breasts firm up,
and icicle summer takes the shoulders.
Now there is a body of winter,
snowmelt necklace around the throat,
and out in the air, only the head,
old basket of everything,
and the gray hair, bush of fog lightning.
And now, take a breath, and take that
air with its pheromones of fallen pine needles
down into the enormous chamber,
the upside-down mountain range of your childhood,
your eyes open, seeing into the

bands, the stripes, of creation, yellow-green,
turquoise, cobalt, indigo, slate,
the elements from which matter will be made,
and then—surfacing rushing gasping—
throw yourself back.

this is just to say

(note left in Room 1724 of the Indianapolis Hilton)

that the pores
in the pear
are not just
in the skin

glossy
and pink-golden
but in the epidermis,
under the epithelium.

I left you the twenty
because I have extra
and I left you the truffles
because I am fat,

but I left you the pear
because it is perfect.
Even more than wanting to eat it
I wanted you to have it.

To Chase, After the Diagnosis

Visible through the stove's glass door,
a log lies, unburning, so I open the
flue, and small flames begin to go on,
like lights in a house in the middle of the night,
until the fire is wild hair.
Dear friend, whose clipped tomboy cap
springs from that shapely head, the surgeons
will make their careful, clean way
inside you, through the locks, through
the doors, chamber by chamber, until
they come to the room with the intruder, and they will
remove it, and test it, and know if they have to
remove, in turn, the furniture
from the room, and the books from the shelves, and the shelves
from the walls, and the walls from the struts, to take you
down to the frame of your next score
of years with us, with the dogs, and the foxglove
and the purple carrots, and the mosses and ferns,
and the granite sluiceways in the wilderness
at the upper lake, and the streams in those creeks
which all your life have run beside you
like napes under your palms, like the gray
hounds accompanying Artemis as she
speeds, fleet, alert, between the trees.

To Chase, During Her Surgery

Above me, outside, between the window and the eave,
there's a spider walking on the sky—walking upside
down, with finicky steps, as if the sky
is sticky, like a kitchen floor
on pie-baking day. Are you in surgery still, do the
surgeons seem on their backs, on the upside-down
ceiling, are you floating, prone, above them?
I know, you are supine, you are opened up,
layer by layer, incision by incision, their
knives and forks and threads and needles are the
anthers and filaments and stigmas and styles
sprouting from within you, like their gloved hands,
their arms enormous stamens and pistils,
and with their magnified eyes and gauze
clothes they're like giant insects, hovering,
drawn to your need, as to the scent
of a *Nymphaea odorata,*
and to the problem of your intricate
geometry, and to the mortal housekeeping
puzzle inside you. From the center of the web,
a smaller spider started walking
down in my direction—then leaped toward me,
from the inner surface of the pane. With the scooping
motion of a night-blooming flower closing,
I got it in a handkerchief
and took it to the porch, and it belayed down
into the garden. The flowers on the hanky were in
full, imaginary bloom, and the garden
still dust and ash, dried leaf and dirt
flecked with quartz in the sun—like constel-
lations, guarded by the dog star, shining
up from inside the ground.

All of a Sudden, I See, and My Heart Sinks

When the downy perches
lengthwise along the broomstick
the suet feeder is hanging from,
I suddenly understand they are
my favorites—the downies and hairies and chickadees,
and the spider smaller than a droplet of water in the
lifted-up ground of the woodsflower nosegay—my
familiars, they are what a child might have
for imaginary family.
I feel *struck down* with the truth of it.
They are my kin, the minuscule songbirds,
and the golden-greenish woodpeckers,
the heron walking her counterclockwise
oval down inside the bank of the pond,
pulling her long, black toes
back, and up, slowly, through the
murk of late summer. I am at home
with them, as if I'd chosen them
as my deepest cohort—as if my mother,
when she beat on me, had driven me
away from the human, toward the avian,
given me to them as Jesus gave John
to Mary. And therefore I don't really live
alone but with the wing ones and the six-legs,
and the eight-legs—and the mammals with dark
claws at the bends of their wings—I want to cry
out, "I have
real children,"
but I spend more time, now, with the flying
reptiles and the lepidopts and the
arachnid falling like a green tear through the
late summer wild Mother's Day bouquet.

What I Look Like

When I was a small child, I thought I was
not very visible—
when I danced with a flower, I was mirroring it,
blossom face, leaves arms,
stem torso, roots legs
and toes. I would cavort and curvet
and twirl-cajole around my mother's
garden, to honor the finger-length entirely
invisible faeries. I wore dresses, and hand-me-down
cardigans of my sister's, the gaps between
the buttoned buttons were pointed ovals
in which the smocked floral pattern of the
dress twisted. But the older I got,
and the more my mother turned me half
upside down to slash at me
for her pleasure, the more troubled my face got—
a shocked look, bleak and ashamed,
sullen, *sollein*, alone.
By the time I was 12, I thought I looked
like a monster—demonstrating my soul's
warp. But when I was 15, boys suddenly
liked me—I loved that,
I knew it was for my body, and despite
my face. But when I turned 70,
I began to think I was pretty, for an older
woman. Not criminally pretty, like
my mom, with those turquoise-blue, faceted
irises, but not disgusting-
looking, and the white world treated me the way it
treated a white, middle-class,
able-bodied woman. How easy I had it.

Now I'm better at talking to people without
thinking my face makes them want to throw up.
I feel I look like what I am—a teacher, a
middle-class WASP, an old dancer, prettyish, beaten by her
    mother.

Dream Near the End

I wake up supine
under the earth
and sense the whole
sphere of it
above my back.   Gravity
is holding my spine   up to the bed,
and holding the bed   up to the floor, and
holding the building   up to the ground which is
above me, like a ceiling   lifted
a little, at its sides, by   the curve of the orb—
our planet, floating, in the   air. I'm awake,
and in my sleep I was writing, underground,
in a squared chamber dug into the topsoil—
the floor dirt, the walls dirt—
and above the hole was a grassy knoll
and Galway was up there, writing, and when we
finished our poems, we would read them to each other.
But then I can't find him,
I climb out of the ground and go up the hill to the house,
to make us coffee—
but everything is wrong,
the grounds are wet and cold and upside
down in the garbage, as if a turned-over
flowerpot has been lifted off its humus,
and there are no poems, there is no Galway,
it is after the end of the world,
and everything is useless—life is useless,
and love useless, sex useless,
and birth useless, and death, itself, now useless.

5
Elegies

PART ONE

Transformations

Her brother became a doctor, like their father.
I would walk to her house every day, after school,
and sit on her bed. She was sick, but not catching.
I knew nothing. I didn't know
her grandma was dead—her father's mother—
and her mother was dead, too, from the lead
paint they had sprayed the fir with in the closed
garage, and my friend, her hair dead-straight and
greenish, like tarnish on old paint
on angels' heads, would be dead in a week
or so, no children at the funeral.
Then her father came to our school, and the girls in our
class went to the Principal's, where
I had been sent, often, to lie down
in the Nurse's Office, because I was so
bad they thought I was crazy. He gave
one of her Storybook Dolls to each
of the girls in her class—the doctor who had
lost his wife, his mother, his daughter,
in a week. Then he reached into the bag, and brought out
her best doll, and said something,
and gave it to me. I felt bad that I felt
proud, and now a strange fear
comes to me—how long had we been
best friends before she died? Years,
I think, but am I sure it was she
who wanted me there every day
or I who wanted to be there. It was

both. I slept with that doll—though her plastic
feet and hands were painful, and her parched
net skirt scratched—until my mother
moved, and my box of things was lost,
like my darling, I had not even been there when she vanished.

Her Brother

I don't think I wanted to "marry him
when I grew up," her elder brother,
I don't think I wanted to marry—I was like
an archery bow of Diana, only
very slightly curved.
I was 9. I don't remember her dwindling
and goldening, but when I looked up their address,
on the net, I knew the window of her bedroom,
facing east—right turn and up
the stairs, right turn and through her door,
each day after school—her parents' and brother's rooms
facing the Bay. The house looked
like a cake, made in a royal bakery
in Paris France, the curved-scale
tiles of the roof like ripples of frosting
squeezed out of the bag with an X
like a cross at the tip of the nozzle. O my darling,
you were 9. How long did it take you to die,
after glazing that Xmas tree silver
with lead paint? Longer than your mother.
I think you curled up, more and more,
dearest soldier.
In the archives, I found your story in the upper
corner of a newspaper for
1953, the amount
a judge awarded your father IN YULE
DEATH. I was looking for news of your brother—I had
never thought of marrying him till I was
78, he'd be 82
or so—but I found he'd been murdered years
later, in his car outside his home.
I had wanted to lie in his room, with him,
skin to skin within sight of the ancient

fresh sun in ridges of western
wind on the water leading out
to the sea, and in, and out. I never got to
hold her, or even to think, Whithersoever
thou goest, there I will be with thee also.

Confessional (for S.B.)

I have been wondering if I am a bully.
I like it when people listen to me.
I love it when animals do.
The night in Washington Square Park,
that long conversation with a mockingbird.
I was not craving attention,
I longed to be accepted as a fellow creature.
When her slayer was digging her grave,
our classmate might have still been in his car,
or lying on the ground like someone asleep in the woods,
on the slope of the coastal hills—fog, salt,
cold air coming out of the mouth of a cave.
The dirt floor of his basement took in her training bra.
He had offered her a ride, she was alone, she was no longer a
    child, almost a young woman.
Where was his soul, he had lost it like an overcoat
dropped in a crowd running through an earthquake.
He drove her over the Hayward Fault,
its boundaries jammed together like an overjaw clenched to an
    underjaw.
When she had not come home to her mother and father and
    sister
they looked for her continually, on land and shore and water.
Her bra lay under his house like a pair of wings buried.
When they found it, they found him and held on to him to kill
    him.
The year before, I had gone waterskiing within sight of Alcatraz,
I hoped I looked cool. I knew nothing.
And today I know almost nothing.
I know you were clean, Stephanie, and smart, and good,
and belonged only to yourself, and to those who loved you.

That Goddess

When I said to the therapist, I'm feeling kind
of calm, but there's a sort of emptiness, as if
something's missing, but I don't know what it is—
he said, Maybe that's mourning, you're mourning
that goddess you thought your mother was,
the one who—if only you'd been lovable—
would have loved you. And I could see her, a columbine
in scarlet and gold empress robes with
pagoda shoulders. And though you could not
possess a goddess, you could glimpse her, a swallow,
aimed as a pair of eighth notes, ravenous.
The universe had not been meaningless—
giant ants rushed with her smoothness,
her chip-of-jet scepters. And at times
of high wind, it would stand and shudder
all over, the vertical sea of her green
aspen dress with its thousands of flashing breasts.
Some things were almost too big to be her,
but I had been inside my mother,
and looked up, and seen the blue-black
vault of her viscera above me sparkling with gallstones.
And her unseen existences,
each small mammal royally pettable, each
strokable coat of each carnivore, each
burrowful of the blind wild young.
The earth was holy. Water in the wind
wrote her. She did not like me, but I was
her daughter, child of the snake and the egg,
of the spectrum and the orb spider—
I, unholy and unblessable,
the spawn of a queen, who rode, without
her body, across the arc of space, not
looking this way, her eyes, behind their

ashy patches, rolled back into her head, she was
seeing the endless emptiness beyond us.
When my mother was a fresh corpse, still
moist, still in translation's magic,
it was as if she'd escaped, leaving us
holding the clothing of her flesh. My mother's
love, the absence of my mother's love,
meant the world to me—this
world, in which I wasted my life
on the ecstasy of craving.

Wasn't Afraid Of

It's funny I wasn't afraid of my mother
after she was dead—an hour after.
It's strange to me. As she'd done her long,
complex dying, breathing, not breathing,
the baby rattle, the diamondback rales, her
face moistening as if lifting into
a low cloud, or lowering,
over a stove, a kettle for a steamer, God's
kitchen towel over her head—as she had
died, and died, she was bringing me close to
our species at its nuptials
with its dying. I held her, circled in my arm—
not to hold her back—and yet
how could she go—as if the blue-wreathed
planet itself were departing, and I was
standing on something, waving to our home as it got
smaller. And then, there she was,
the material object, and yet fresh
as a fresh-born baby released from the sea
of the womb. Who could have feared the new, the
sparse motionless soldier of her.
And an hour later, once I had turned
away, and come back, she wasn't at all like the
night-terrors figure who used to hover
above me in my bed, before sleep. Dead,
her forehead did assume a faint
shell of garden-snail look, but she was
nothing like my bedroom's airborne prone night-
hecate with the leaking face.
No longer. She was gone to where
they cannot scare you, anymore.
And no one, now, stood between me

and my life—unless there was a small figure
taking shape in me, like the scepter on
the hospice gurney. From now on,
it couldn't be my mother who was fearsome to me.
It would have to be me.

Looking for Galway
on the Vermont Mountainside

The overcast was complete, except for
a small rip, to the east, where steam was
breathing through, glacier blue.
The world was soaked, I climbed uphill
in undersea shoes, waded through sop
clover, blossoms spittled with rain like
egg-cases of fishing spiders who
carry their unborn in bubbles in their mouth.
There were patches where hay showed through the wild grasses,
    there were
smooth declivities, where a deer or
bear might have lain down. But I could not
find the grave. Where *are* you, I cried out,
under my breath, where are you. I was not
a mother who has lost her child in a crowd,
I was never, to him, a mother, always
like an aunt, though younger, warm but stern,
but not a sister, not family—
a stranger, a fellowe stranger. For a moment
I thought I would not find him, that he'd gone
back by means of the periodic
table to his component elements,
and then, as I rose, dew-booted, the top of the
hill began
to rise slowly
above the top of the hill—the slate
table, and beyond it, on the brow of the mountain,
the dolmen of granite, like a column of ancient
rough flesh, and will, and at
his foot a flat rock, like an open
book. Joe Pye weed, rich dirt,
bladder campion—"You're a garden!"

I said to my best friend, and took up
a little roundish golden rock—
"Can I borrow this?"—
from the turned soil, and put it on
his footstone. The ions in the air were bouncing
like fine sprinkle, and the bud scales and
spiracles of the young tree
planted near him were gold against the ruddy,
smooth, amber, elm bark,
I gripped and kissed the tree, I gripped and
kissed the tough, bright-specked maul of the
metamorphic stone, and descended
the latch-mat stairs and bared my feet
down to the chilled skin, and found in the
laundry basket a couple of big
socks without mates, and I accepted them
as gifts—one a gray with a band of
acid green on its toe, its nose,
one a wool heather of moss
and brown and honey, with touches of scarlet
and black. In his socks, I am jubilant,
I think of who I will bequeath them to,
when I am under
your bootsoles with him—
whoever you are, holding me now in hand.

Suddenly

(Ruth Stone, June 8, 1915–November 19, 2011)

And suddenly, it's today, it's this morning
they are putting Ruth into the earth,
her breasts going down, under the hill,
like the moon and sun going down together.
O I know it's not Ruth—what was Ruth
went out, slowly, but this was her form,
beautiful and powerful
as the old, gorgeous goddesses who were
terrible, too, not telling a lie
for anyone—and she'd been left here so long, among
mortals, by her mate—who could not,
one hour, bear to go on being human.
And I've gone a little crazy myself
with her going, which seems to go against logic,
the way she has always been there, with her wonder, and her
generousness, her breasts like two
voluptuous external hearts.
I am so glad she kept them, her whole
life, and she got to be buried in them—
she, 96, and they
maybe 82
each, which is
164 years
of pleasure and longing. And think of all
the poets who have suckled at her riskiness, her
risqué, her body politic, her
outlaw grace! What she came into this world with,
with a mew and cry, she gave us. In her red
sweater and her red hair and her raw
melodious Virginia crackle,
she emptied herself fully out

into her songs and our song-making,
we would not have made our songs without her.
O dear one, what is this? You are not a child,
though you dwindled, you have not retraced your path,
but continued to move straight forward to where
we will follow you, radiant mother. Red Rover, cross over.

After Reading *Shallcross*

(for C.D., and Forrest)

1

When I was reading your poem, seeing your character
whole, bright as granite, not hap-
hazard but improv elegant,
I felt unworthy to write you, I started to feel
low, then I hugged your book, and cried out, *I am*
blessed, I am blessed, I am blessed, I am blessed,
flooded with the fortune of having known you and been
known by you,
and I kissed your book, hard, feeling
the strength of my mouth—not hard as in difficult, I don't
think of myself as difficult—
that's my folly, my dishonor, to think
I'm easy. It was not hard for my husband
to leave me. What had been hard, for him,
after the first thirty years, was
to be with me—easy for his body,
I did not know that had little, for him,
anymore, to do with love.
It felt, to me, like love itself,
which is just to say how little I knew.
But one thing I know is that one of the things,
after he left me, that reconciled me
to myself, was you, Carolyn,
who could see me as I was, and see me as true enough—
breasts that pressed against other breasts it was you!

2

P.S., I also like the physical
body of your book—wide-opened, face-entered,
it smells like the clean inside of a tree. When I was
stood in the corner, I would smell the corner,
the hard, right
angle of it,
coming to odor grips with the Calvinists
who'd made me. Stucco, Republican adobe,
equilateral, cold—I was always
cold in Northern California,
and I didn't know I felt anger. Half
a century later, my rage rose up as if
out of a New Hampshire floor, taking the
power of my knees, as I said to Carl,
"I do not agree with you." And as I
stroke your book, Carolyn,
it warms to my touch—not those newfangled
rubberized boards, but a solid, smooth
cardboard cover. We walked, in Berkeley, till we
stood under
the copper beech
in what had been my mother's garden,
and over my shoulder you saw the neighbor's
face open and light up as mine did when I
turned. *Cara*, I'm so glad I could present you to

Elena e Elio—*"una grande poeta*
americana di Arkansas!"
My mother, who seemed to feel virtuous as Virgil,
had showed me what life could be, if you lacked
what, the love of a mother, which my mother
herself had lacked. I showed you her beech,
her redwood, her sequoia, her espaliered pear, and you had—
what can I call them—the visionary balls,
cojones de madre, to love me. I feel as if
I owe you my life. If you—our best, in your
fresh, saltwater wit—could stand me,
how bad could I be? Never to have not
been with thee. Never not those moments.

PART TWO

When They Say You Have Maybe
Three Months Left

In my sleep, I dreamed that I came to your grave—
and what lay between us? The beautiful uncut
hair of the grass, and topsoil like the rich
dirt in which you buried our sheets
after I left you—our DNA—near where
you later buried your golden dog.
Also between us the new ceiling
of plain pine, and the linen garment
your fresh-washed unbreathing body had been clothed in,
and the earthen chamber music of wild,
underworld, spiral creatures,
and your tissue I have loved, and within it the ancient
primordial man of your skeleton.
Narwhal tusk, elephant ivory,
icon of your narrow-hipped male power
I rode, rowing in eden. But
it was no dream, I lay broad waking,
and you have not died yet. I can read this to you
in a week, in front of the woodstove,
the flames curving up to points and disappearing,
or beside the pond, the water rippling,
ovals of hemlock and beech changing places in it.
Sometimes you fall asleep as I'm talking to you.
And you've said: I want you to be reading me a poem when I die.
And, Let's not stop writing to each other when I'm dead.
And when I'm dead too! I said. When we met,
though we fell in love immediate and permanent,
we could not make a two-soul union,

nor when I left—each of us had to
work, on ourselves, for years, to get there.
And now we are there! Maybe this has been
death all along! Maybe life is a
kind of dying. Maybe *this* has been heaven.

Heroin

In an old mystery, someone is
returning, to a pharmacy,
the heroin her relative had not needed
before he died. I look up—
it's night already—and ask myself, did I
really give Carl heroin?
Sometimes, when I was alone with him
for a weekend, the hospice nurses on call—
yes! heroin was the one
measured with the dropper, and given, to him,
under his tongue.
Even now, a year later,
a laugh bursts out of me when I remember
the time my tremor spoiled my aim,
and he barked, "*Under* my tongue! That wasn't
under my tongue!" I like remembering
the vital ghost of the temper in him, and how it
felt being alone, in sleep-time, in the woods,
in the house with him, how dark outside,
how warmly lit by the woodstove and the
lanterns' isinglass, and those thin-carved
golden shades like salad bowls upside
down which showed the ovals of the grain.
It had been fifty years since I'd been
alone in a house with a newborn—and I'd
hardly known how to care for her—
but now I had the charts for the heroin and
morphine for his pain and anxiety.
And we seemed to be in an enormous world,
which began even more than 5780
years ago, one which would never
end—and once it ended, it would always
have been, kisses and all—oh those tender kisses!

When the Cancer Has Come Back,
Sleeping in His House with Him
but Not in His Bed with Him

And in the night, each time I woke,
the sheet and mattress were level and sweet, I
put my trusting as-if-good-child cheek
down, again, on the surface of sleep.
And when my eyes opened once more,
across from me, through the big clean
glass, was the sky, as if colorless, with so many
tiny lights of so many bright
hues, golden, violet,
the pine pure black at night, two or three
hundred years old, and the sky bright
with hundreds, or thousands, of tiny lights,
gray, ivory, golden, violet,
I, at length, facing the dark
fellow horizontal of the hills—
to my left, the sky; the snow-covered lake
to my right; as if I were a dragon or damsel
fly, one wing of overcast,
one of frozen snow over ice over
water which, from underwater, is
golden with mica and pollen in summer
—my body, my life, a pulse of earth.
And sometimes the small motion-bulb
in the hall would glow, as he passed by
from his bed to the stove, to throw in,
with his accurate arm, a split of wood then
push its near end with his slipper almost
gently, to encourage it toward
the heat which before we went to our sleeps
was incandescent,
rose orange, flower and food

of heat. And when the sensor would flick on,
I'd watch the lumen upright crack
between the door and its frame, to see
his bulk, now large and slow, pass,
like watching a spirit. Then I pulled
the down cover
up over
my chin, and a part at the top rose,
and unfolded over my face, like a curl of
dirt taking me into the ground.
Then I came to the window and sat, under the
eave where the barred owl would cry out
in sovereign peace or in longing, and now
I sit where I used to sit—as if
alone in the world, which I am not, and look
out at the land of which he is the
guardian, in perpetuity,
and watch as first
light comes
slow, the milky surface, where we
saw, in the cold, two coyotes cavort,
screaming—half tail, half dog, like us,
and, in the heat wave, where we'd sunk below
the surface of Wild Goose, we'd look at
each other's bodies, golden with silt,
not as if external, and not
as if, but in true, difficult love.

His Birthday

When I'm in New York and he's in New Hampshire, and I'm
starting to make love to myself,
on his birthday, I look around for something
silky, as I'd rubbed the satin binding of my
childhood blanket when I'd sucked my thumb
to sleep, until I was 13 and had
buck teeth. On his 75th,
I wanted to caress myself
through something which had a glimmery feeling.
And when I came, the first time,
it almost picked me up and threw me
off the bed. Resting, I panted,
like the pleasure-wounded. And the second time,
the blunt force of it was so
deep it made me think of the crump
of fireworks, the full chrysanthemum
in each chamber of the sex's heart.
After the third time, my hand hung
down off the side of the mattress as if by a
thread, like a spider dropping down
to affix a hypotenuse for a web,
and after the fourth, for a while I could not
open my left eye, sun
green around the rim like a pond
at noon. He is alive! He is 75!
I lie in liminal dishevel, the sweet
remains of a birthday party, spiral
honeybee candles, with black wicks—
the taffeta ribbons, the many happy returns.

His Voice, a Week Before His Spirit Follows His Voice Out

When it's been a few days since I have
heard his voice, when I call him I start
laughing with happiness, to hear
the known, low, male burr—not
monotone, but melody,
resonance—and the more exhausted
he is, the more fur sound,
the rough mammal with a coat both rough
and smooth, curly, wavy, hoarse,
talking to me! With his tremor, he can't
type, and now he can't really
use a fork—a straw is good,
or spoon-fed. Before we hang up,
I say, I am alone here,
and I know there are folks there now, so I can say
I love you so much, and you can just say
Goodbye. *Soon!* he says, and I say
Yes, laughing, as lovers may laugh.
O.K., see ya! he says, and I say,
See ya! laughing, my arteries seeding with
oxygen of laughter like blown
dandelion seeds—the luck of true love!
The radiance of preference, mutual and equal.

Three Views of Him Asleep, His Final Days

One was through the wooden-framed doorway
of the guest room—I was resting on an old,
heavy, oak, Stickley, bed, my
nape held up by the footboard cross-piece—
now I look back, I think I was like
a present, in its box, he would wake soon
and call my name and I'd emerge, his girl
from inside a cake. The head of his hospice
bed was hummed up, I saw the curve of his
great, domed forehead, creamy
cancer color, like a five-night moon
setting, points down, below it the
dark, tear-drop shape of his nostrils, and, be-
low them, his mouth open
in sleep, his head framed in the wild
silver and black which started to come back
in when the chemo was stopped, not round but
ellipsis ripples which will keep growing
when he's bedded down in the unending night
in which we believe he will not be lonely.
Two was when the long bristles of the
coarse coat of his beard were level with my
eyes, he on his back asleep
in the bed on wheels, I on my side,
fitted to him between the laid-low
mountain of his body and the guard-rail at my back—
cradle bars, training-bed,
training grave. Three was later,
he at my left, the fire dying
to my right, me beneath the hot
coal-color parchment of the iron lamp,
reading as he slept, his golden animal
familiar, Witch Hazel, not entirely

gone from the living room yet. The wood
stove, the good dog, the flexible
bed with its branches—a tree I know well
how to climb—
and the fine, worn man almost hori-
zontal a couple of feet above
the layers of carpets, the home-hewn floor,
the cellar ceiling, yards above
the basement porch, another yard
above the complex dirt of the earth,
resting on its stone and iron,
each of us a companion, as he
does his dying, the last hard work of his life.

The Preparing

Only after the years, months, of our
talks about what dying is—
he felt no one could meet his eyes
when they knew he would die, soon (*Shhh,*
no one but I)—
only after he had died, did I see I'd been
all my life, preparing to help him—as a
child I had recited it weekly,
Yea, though I walk through the valley of the shadow
of death, thou art with me—fuck thy rod and thy
staff—Carl who had got in a fight
once, as a boy, and hated the way it
felt to hurt someone. He loved
that I was not mean, I was actually gentle—
if it went over into syrupy,
he would *hok* me. Only I—only
this one who had left him, and come back as his soul-mate—
could he joke with about coffin worms.
Month after month, his horror of death
decreased. When everyone was out of the house I'd
jungle-gym up into the hospice trough—he could
no longer move—
and jam myself, softly, in
sideways between the gaunt mountain
of him, and the rail, and we'd choke up, for a moment,
with relief, and then we'd be asleep
for an hour of the imaginary
serene. Imagine being able
to calm the one you love best,
who loves you best,
I had never thought it would come to that, though I'd been
practicing, marching up and

down the redwood decks of that small
boat of a church—speaking, as if I was
Carl speaking to me: Yo, though I
walk through the valley of the shadow of death,
I shall fear no evil, for thou art with me.

The Box

The long, pale box of unfinished
pine had a pink branch, with bark,
for a strong handle, running along each
side—up each side, from the dear,
icy cold, naked feet,
to his head, at peace for the first time
since his conception. There was a pair of brown
knotholes in the side facing us,
and lines of grain in rivulets.
After the shepherd, the want, the green
pastures, the lid looked loose to me a moment,
as if the six-point New Hampshire pine
star rose and fell, and then
they wheeled my darling down the, up the
aisle on the trolley's crisscross legs
and wheels, to the deep rectangle
dug, straight down, with clean edges—
black layer of topsoil, then the
sheer faces of dirt, tree rootlets
breaking out into the air like delicate
worms. And the Rabbi called out, as if
in grief, Chaim Ben Ephraim!—and the
beautiful man traveled, without
moving, back into the earth he had come from, and had
made his first cry of his own.
The first back-of-the-shovel drop
of dirt onto that beautiful box, that
beautiful boy, was an awful sound,
but then the scoops of sandy soil
began to sound like the work of our kind,
honorable, requiring deep
breath and sweat. I took some, from the pile, and put my
hand in my pocket and rubbed my fingers

and thumb, laying up treasure. Then I
plucked a dead cello string from a
red pine so it would not scratch the Rabbi's
hat, and then I saw they had put a
little sign on a stick in the crown
of the mound, like an upside-down flower-seed packet,
to say what is there, with his name on it like
Snowdrop, Double Bloodroot, Closed Gentian.

After an Epitaph on an English Headstone

I count myself blessed that I did not have to
go through your death in the presence of God.
In our presence there was only the God who had chosen
your people, he had been there in your father's and mother's
house, and we had kept to the candles
and the braided bread, to the principle
that your life was precious. No God but yours
was there with us, any more than one might
surbed a coal upright on a fire
or a granite stone on a grave. You died
an animal of the land and water, where we'd
swayed naked, carrot-golden, its
ripples like the shirring of surah silk,
as you went into the ground in a linen slip.
After the hormones you felt you might not be
a man, anymore. I said, you are a man
who has learned about women from the outside in
and inside out, the chemo had loosed you from some
sir-like bonds, some male ions,
as well as from the bonds of sexual joy.
You still shaved your powerful, eloquent
face—I would touch my lips to your bristle—
and now your beard is growing without sun
in the lightless place, but let no one say
you slipped the surly bonds of earth
to touch the face of God—the gods
of the elements had slipped the bonds of nothing to create you.

Can't Sleep

Turning one cheek, then
the other, to the cool sheet,
I remember long-legging up onto your
hospice cot, and pulling the railing up
after me, like a tree-house ladder.
How we rode that cloud, its low heaven,
murmuring our naked truths,
kissing then sleeping. You could no longer move,
just your hands and a little your head,
turning it partway and pushing your lips
my way when you wanted my mouth. I was not there
at the end, my darling, but sometimes now
I pretend to magic myself down
into your coffin, along you, and love your
soul with my soul. It was violent
to see them set you, Carl Michael,
into the excavation so deep I could
not see the raw pine
roof Nik created for you until I
edged closer. When I can't sleep I
get my back against the grain home-kilned at the
staging—along your right side—
you, stretched out, a mighty dancer
at rest, planted in a freeze, thawing now.
Whenever I see a scene, on film,
underground—a narrow stone passage
with lights coming forward through it, up,
up, till we see one light is on a brow
and the other its reflection in the water,
I feel they're honoring you,
your beauty and courage being turned to earth,
slowly given back. I told you I would
find you, gorgeous one, I *told* you.

Komodo

When I saw, on the floor, back in the unlighted
pantry, the forgotten trap, with a scribble of
small mammal under it—maybe
smallest mammal: bumblebee bat;
pocket monkey; pygmy jerboa;
Etruscan shrew; hog-nosed bat—
I said to myself, I'll empty it tomorrow,
open the plastic jaws and drop
the little steaks and chops with limbs onto a
piece of tinfoil on the carriage stone.
The next day, the day after,
by the time I carried it outside, my tremor
wiggled it, as if it were struggling—
and the mouse was caught in two traps, like a
valentine heart, so I lowered it into
a bucket, and put it on the porch step, and it
rained more, so I opened the traps and
dropped the carousel of worms
in the woods, the biggest larva the length of the
mouseling's head. In quarantine
isolation, I'd had a thought
of you, my darling, and backed up from the thought:
if our corpses attracted necromancers
of comparable size to the mouse's, my love would have
a Komodo dragon in his grave with him.
Oh my darling, forgive me, are you a skeleton
yet? 28 weeks, someone said, when it's
above freezing. When you died, you arrived at the
feast table, and your throne, and after
the banquet, we went to your four-poster bed,
each post a tree—oak, beech,

hemlock, pine—and have been resting together
at the end of the festival. What's strange to me
this morning, is that I think you still
love me, even though I've written this.
Love is the love of who we are, it is a form of knowing.

Sharon Olds was born in San Francisco and educated at Stanford University and Columbia University. She is the recipient of the Frost Medal for lifetime achievement, as well as the winner of both the Pulitzer Prize and England's T. S. Eliot Prize for her 2012 collection, *Stag's Leap*. She is the author of twelve previous books of poetry and the winner of other awards and honors, including the inaugural San Francisco Poetry Center Award for her first book, *Satan Says* (1980), and the National Book Critics Circle Award for her second, *The Dead and the Living*, which was also the Lamont Poetry Selection for 1983. *The Father* was short-listed for the T. S. Eliot Prize, and *The Unswept Room* was a finalist for the National Book Award and the National Book Critics Circle Award. Olds teaches in the Graduate Creative Writing Program at New York University and helped to found the NYU outreach programs, among them the writing workshop for residents of the former S. S. Goldwater Hospital on Roosevelt Island, and for the veterans of the Iraq and Afghanistan wars. She lives in New York City.

A NOTE ON THE TYPE

The text of this book was set in a typeface called Bell. The original punches for this face were cut in 1788 by the engraver Richard Austin for the typefoundry of John Bell (1745–1831), the most outstanding typographer of his day. They are the earliest English "modern" type design, and show the influence of French copperplate engraving and the work of the Fournier and Didot families. However, the Bell face has a distinct identity of its own, and might also be classified as a delicate and refined rendering of Scotch Roman.

Composed by North Market Street Graphics,
Lancaster, Pennsylvania

Printed and bound by Berryville Graphics,
Berryville, Virginia

Designed by Soonyoung Kwon